Getting Our Childhood

How Adults Can Recover from Trauma That Began at School

Stacey J. Miller

BPT Press

RANDOLPH, MA

Copyright © 2018 by Stacey J. Miller

All rights reserved. No part of this publication may be reproduced, distributed or transmitted in any form or by any means, without prior written permission.

Printed in the United States of America

First printing, 2018

BPT Press
For queries: bookpromotion@gmail.com
http://sjmiller23.wixsite.com/bullying

Publisher's Note: This is a work of nonfiction. Some names and identifying details have been changed to protect the privacy of individuals.

Book Layout © 2014 BookDesignTemplates.com

Getting Past Childhood Bullying: How Adults Can Recover From Trauma That Began at School / Stacey J. Miller -- 1st ed.

ISBN 978-0-9842285-3-9

Disclaimer

The information provided within this book is for general informational purposes only and is based on the author's personal experiences. This book is not intended to be a substitute for the medical advice of a licensed physician or mental health professional. The intent of the author/publisher is only to offer information of a general nature to help you in your quest for emotional and spiritual well-being. In the event that you use any of the information in this book for yourself, which is your constitutional right, the author/publisher assume no responsibility for your actions. The reader should consult with a doctor or mental health professional in any matters relating to his/her physical and mental health, respectively.

Dedication

To Mathilde Andrade,
Anna Rinaldi, Johnna Chastang, and Marianne Lacey

Thank you for being my salvation.

CONTENTS

PREFACE 1
INTRODUCTION 3
BULLYING COMES OUT OF THE CLOSET 7
A 4-PART PROGRAM TO GET PAST THE TRAUMA 11
   The 4-Part Program 13
   Proceed With Caution 15
MY STORY 17
   At Junior High School 17
   The Day of the Funeral 29
   The Loss of Phoebe Prince 37
A NEW PERCEPTION OF BULLYING 41
   Defining Bullying 43
HEALING FROM THE PAST 45
THE REASONS FOR SILENCE 51
TELLING YOUR STORY, PART 1 55
   Beginning Your Narrative 58
   The Characters 59
TELLING YOUR STORY, PART 2 113
   Informal Approach 115
   Traditional Approach 121
OPTIMIZE YOUR ONLINE PRESENCE 137
FINDING YOUR FOES ONLINE 151
   Shrinking the Monsters 152

Beginning Your Search 156

Search for Your Foes Online 160

Finding Bad News Online 193

The People You Don't Choose to Find 194

FACING YOUR FOES IN THE REAL WORLD 197

The Case of Dr. Lance Hindt 198

Weighing the Pros and Cons 201

Taking the Next Steps 202

AFTERWORD 229

ACKNOWLEDGEMENTS 237

ABOUT THE AUTHOR 239

PREFACE

It is March of 2017. A notification pops up on my cell phone from a Facebook group, "You know you're from Simmet [not the city's actual name] when...."

I click on the icon, and I see a photo of Simmet High School, or what remains of it.

There's a wide, ugly hole in the building that a wrecking ball has left behind. The demolition of the early twentieth century red brick school was underway when the picture was taken, but there's enough left of the building's structure to fill me with emotion.

That building held a lot of my family history. My parents, sisters, grandparents, and many of my cousins (and second cousins), aunts, and uncles (and great-aunts and great-uncles) had graduated from Simmet High School.

My maternal great-uncle had taught biology there, and my oldest sister had been his student. She adored him. For years, she shared stories about how our great-uncle had playfully tossed dead bugs at sleepy students to wake them up. According to family folklore, all of Uncle Aaron's students loved him, too. He was one of their favorite teachers. They even dedicated their high school yearbook to him posthumously.

The mythology of the school, including the characters that made up its faculty, the school's teams, its jackets, and even its mascot, had always been part of my world.

One day, I'd attend Simmet High School. That was more than my dream. It was my legacy. I was supposed be part of the Simmet High School graduating class of 1981.

Except that, for a crazy set of reasons, it never happened.

Since the first few days of my junior high school experience, I'd known that it shouldn't happen. At a soul level, I had understood that it *mustn't* happen.

Bullying at the hands of my junior high school classmates, in conjunction with the neglect and incompetence exhibited by the teachers and administrative members of that junior high school, had made it seem impossible for me to attend the local public high school.

Everyone involved in the fiasco that was my junior high school experience had made it clear that I would have been neither safe nor welcome at Simmet High School.

So I didn't attend Simmet High School. It seemed my survival depended on giving up that fantasy. However, my clear understanding that I was making the only possible choice didn't quell my longing to be there every hour of every day that I attended another high school instead.

As the years passed, my feelings of loss faded, but they never left me completely. To me, Simmet High School always represented what should have been. It always symbolized my greatest failure and my deepest regret. And I never talked about it with anyone, because I couldn't.

INTRODUCTION

When I was in middle school (except we called it junior high school back then; this was during the years between 1975 and 1977), few people discussed bullying. The fact that some children tormented other children verbally and physically was accepted as a fact of life. For the most part, it was shrugged off as casually as inclement weather. If people had to reference bullying at all, they frequently used the cliché: "It's just kids being kids."

The "just" ensured that no one would blow such a small, ordinary thing out of proportion. Surely, all children were resilient enough to deal with a little bit of bullying.

When you were a target, you sucked it up. (I use the word "target" instead of "victim" by design. Those of us who experienced bullying at school do not have to consider ourselves victims.)

After it ended, one way or another — either because you left the scene of the bullying, or because the bullies became bored with you and shifted their focus onto someone else instead — there was no reason to ever think about it again. The trauma of bullying was expected to simply evaporate, and you were supposed to move on with your life.

No one acknowledged that bullying might have long-term consequences. If you knew differently — say, because you'd been bullied as a child, and you hadn't been able to escape its lasting impact even though you were well into your adulthood — you were supposed to pretend otherwise.

If, years after you'd finished school, you still suffered the residual effects of bullying — for example, emotional fragility; social avoidance; anxiety; sadness; an inability to trust; difficulty with maintaining friendships; micro-bursts of anger and aggression; defensiveness; and lack of self esteem — you probably never acknowledged the origins of those issues, even to yourself.

You felt embarrassed when you weren't prepared to explain the gaps in the autobiographical stories you could tell. But you told yourself that you were just a private person, and there was nothing more to it than that.

Of course, you *might* have acknowledged that there was no great mystery about your childhood. The deep, dark secret was relatively straightforward. You had been targeted by bullies. Bad things had happened, and you would prefer to keep those memories to yourself. It was that simple.

But you most likely didn't do that, because silence was the best coping technique you knew. It was also the only socially acceptable way of dealing with your past.

Bullying was a dirty word for so many years. No one wanted to utter it, and no one wanted to hear it.

The only thing anyone wanted was for you to just forget it had ever happened. That was a good idea all around. It was helpful to you, because it allowed you to save face and hold onto some vestiges of your dignity. It was good for your family, friends and, later, your coworkers, because they didn't have to risk involving themselves in your melodrama. And it probably was best of all for the perpetrators — the children who had bullied you, or had been a part of that bullying, and the adults who had allowed it — because your silence spared them the need to take responsibility for their actions.

Everyone felt most comfortable pretending that bullying was an acceptable rite of passage with no permanent consequences. If anyone was held to blame for bullying, it was the targets who were too weak and ineffectual to fight back. Darwinism was harsh, but it was fair. It was also inevitable. If you couldn't stand up to the bullies, then that was your bad luck and your responsibility. No one owed you, or anybody else, an explanation or apology.

Bullying happened. That was the reality, and that was the end of the discussion.

CHAPTER ONE

BULLYING COMES OUT OF THE CLOSET

Times have changed. In March 2011, United States President Barack Obama confessed at a White House summit called the White House Conference on Bullying Prevention that he was bullied as a child.

The fact that bullying had happened to the President of the United States was a game changer for many of us. Bullying was officially out of the closet. Political pundits discussed it, talk shows raised the subject, journalists wrote about it, schools formed (or took more seriously) anti-bullying task forces, and parents learned to ask their children about it.

Teachers, coaches, and school administrators learned they could no longer normalize it. They discovered there might even be negative consequences for them if they tried.

Those who were targeted by bullies were no longer expected to keep silent and hope it would just go away by itself. The adults who were responsible for them could no longer ignore it with impunity. They could no longer pretend that

8 · STACEY J. MILLER

bullying was acceptable. Conflict resolution was something teachers discussed in the classroom.

Bullying had arrived as a legitimate problem that warranted management tools and preventative techniques. You can find evidence online that people are now taking it seriously. The United States government has an official bullying prevention website, www.StopBullying.gov. Then there is an organization called STOMP Out Bullying™ that has received support from dozens of celebrities and entertainment industry personalities including Billy Joel, Marie Osmond, Elton John, Ellen DeGeneres, and Henry Winkler.

Disney and ABC Television joined forces to create public service announcements featuring Kelly Ripa and Ryan Seacrest as part of an anti-bullying campaign (#ChooseKindness). Lady Gaga launched the Born This Way Foundation to tackle bullying. Finally, it became a trendy enough problem that even socialite-turned-first lady, Melania Trump, launched an anti-bullying campaign of her own and lamented that she saw herself as a target of bullying.

Bullying also made its way into academia. In May 2016, Oxford University Press published a book written by Ellen Walser deLara, PhD, MSW called *Bullying Scars: The Impact on Adult Life and Relationships*. In it, Dr. deLara aptly describes the long-term damage that childhood bullying can cause for some people.

A 2018 United Nations report found that 150 million students between the ages of 13 and 15 — that is, half of all students in that age group — around the world had experienced bullying or violence at school. In other words, schools were not safe places for approximately half of the students who attended them. Children around the world spent their school hours living in fear.

I had plenty of company in experiencing the trauma of bullying. Like so many others, I initially lacked the necessary skills and resources to reduce the amount of residual pain I experienced from bullying.

In my case, I relived the past endlessly, dwelling on the shame, hurt, and fear that I had felt. If I had wanted to, I probably could have recalled much of what had occurred on a moment-to-moment basis. Instead, I suppressed nearly all of the story except for the most egregious events. Those, I replayed over and over again in my mind.

CHAPTER TWO

A 4-PART PROGRAM TO GET PAST THE TRAUMA

What kept me gnawing on the bone was the puzzle of why I had been chosen to receive such terrible mistreatment. What had gone wrong? To what extent was it my fault? What might I have done differently?

I worried about whether I had coping mechanisms in place now to ensure that it could never happen again. In addition, I agonized over whether the fears, insecurities, and defense mechanisms I had developed in response to the treatment I had experienced might be getting in the way of my current, and potential, relationships.

If I had talked openly about my experiences, through the years, it might have been possible for me to process them effectively. Maybe, eventually, they wouldn't have been such a big deal. I might have been able to put them into perspective. They might have lost their melodramatic qualities as time went on and my universe expanded beyond the junior high school where it had all begun.

But, since all the memories and the anguish they caused remained hidden inside of me, the unspoken story of the bullying in my childhood grew disproportionately damaging. The secret's power over me expanded in direct proportion to my inability to talk about it.

My life went on. But, when I least expected it, thoughts of the abuse I'd suffered in my childhood would interfere with my present-day moments, and I'd have to navigate through a tangle of darkness before I could maneuver my way back to the light.

Ruminating about what I perceived to be my past failures was a maladaptive behavior I just couldn't quit. It was like this endless malevolent earworm, and I yearned to find a way to make it stop.

Fortunately, although I am among the many people who were targeted by bullies in my childhood, I eventually found a way to make peace with the past.

I used the tools and strategies you'll read about here to begin the process of making myself feel safe and whole again. These techniques did not provide an instant cure for my childhood trauma. But they did allow me to find closure and move beyond the unremitting pain.

Despite the insistence of everyone that the bullying didn't matter — that it happened to nearly everyone, and there was no reason to dwell on it, because it was no big deal — I recognized that it was a legitimate problem. I acknowledged the gravity of what had occurred to me and its role in shaping the choices I had subsequently made.

Childhood bullying had helped to shape my adult life, and I was finally willing to recognize that.

I took control of the earworm and listened to the entire song. Once I had stopped suppressing the memories of that time in my life, I could deal with them. With that behind me, I was no longer at the mercy of my experiences.

In time, I learned to face the bullying of my childhood and work through the trauma, and so can you. The free fall that began when you were tormented by bullies can end.

You, too, can make peace with your past and move on. That's what this book is about.

Unfortunately, I had to discover, for myself, that denying the past only made things worse. Through trial and error, I developed the program that I used to help myself heal. Facing the past, and all of its demons, became my pathway to letting go.

In the pages that follow, you'll find the program that I used to stop the memories of childhood bullying from endlessly tormenting me. You will also find ideas I gleaned from hearing about the collective experiences of other adults who were the targets of bullying at school.

The 4-Part Program

The program, that I will share with you here, consists of four parts.

First, you tell your story.

Bullying used to be a dirty secret, and you might have played along. You can decide to try a new approach. Allow yourself to remember the parts of your experiences with childhood bullying that feel safe to recall.

The story is yours. Take ownership of it, and tell it to yourself. Then decide whether or not you want to share the story with others.

Second, you maximize your online presence.

The internet has made the world a much smaller place. Chances are, anyone from your past can find you again within just a few minutes without even exerting much effort.

That can be a terrifying prospect unless you take charge of what people will see when they find you online and prepare yourself for the eventuality of their getting in touch.

Third, you find your foes online.

You do not have to wait for people to find you online. Instead, you can find them first. That allows you to put the people associated with the bullying of your childhood into perspective.

You will see that they are not omniscient. They can't hurt you anymore because, after all, they are just ordinary mortals.

Fourth, you face your foes in the real world.

The childhood bullying you experienced might have ended without providing you with an opportunity for closure. You may feel that you still have unfinished business with the people who hurt you.

While you cannot change the past, you can shoot an alternate ending by meeting the people from your past once more when you are ready. Finally, you can end the story on your terms.

Proceed With Caution

These are the four steps I took on the road to healing. Some, or all, of them may help you as well. They will not provide a cure for the trauma of childhood bullying, nor will they create instant happiness.

These steps involve revisiting a horrible part of your past. That can unleash a world of pain. You may find that following this program makes you feel worse than you do now, in the short term, before it provides you with a chance to find healing and peace.

Getting past childhood bullying is not an all-or-nothing proposition. Taking steps toward healing may be the most important gift you can give yourself.

Do not feel pressured into undertaking all four parts of the program. Some aspects of it may feel right to you. Others may not. Stay within your comfort zone.

Proceed sensibly. Read all the parts of the program in advance of plunging in. Seek the advice of your mental health professional if you already are working with one. And, if you are not, then please consider doing so.

Otherwise, tap into the support system that you have available to you. Revisiting a traumatic past is difficult, and no one should have to do it alone. Surround yourself with everything you need to stay hopeful, grounded, and strong.

Finding the peace that you deserve is the goal. Bringing your experience from the darkness into the light is the methodology.

CHAPTER THREE

MY STORY

I was bullied as an 11-, 12-, and 13-year-old. For two school years, during every school day, I was insulted, mocked, ostracized, and threatened. For much of that time, I was physically assaulted on a daily basis. It was more emotionally and spiritually shattering than I can convey to anyone who has not experienced bullying and violence at school.

Even now, it is difficult for me to share my story, and it is rare that I do. However, it seems important to explain my experience with childhood bullying and some of the ways in which its aftermath affected my life, so here is the essence of what happened.

At Junior High School

When I arrived at junior high school for the first time, I was nearly a teenager. I had waited eagerly for that magical moment when I could graduate from my childhood and begin my life as a young woman. To me, it seemed as if I were on the

18 · STACEY J. MILLER

threshold of everything. Physical maturation was my holy grail at the time, and I couldn't wait for it to begin.

Elementary school had been wonderful in just about every way, but junior high school would be even better, because that was the way life was. Every day was better than the one before it. I had so much to look forward to.

Autumn was my favorite time of year, the dipping temperatures notwithstanding, and school had always been a happy place for me. I was an enthusiastic student who loved words and everything related to them. I'd always considered myself a favorite of teachers and the other children.

A new school year at a new school meant new teachers and new classes. I was assigned to a group (called a division) of students who would attend each of those classes with me.

On the first day of school, I had scored a set of gently used textbooks that I couldn't wait to explore. Months before, my parents had supplied me with fresh notebooks just begging to be filled. The start of each school year was always a treat for me, and this September promised to be special because it was the beginning of my junior high school experience.

After seven years of being in a class with the same core of children, it was exciting to have an opportunity to meet a new group of kids. I was so blissful that I think I floated, rather than walked, through the corridors during those first couple of days.

Maybe my enthusiasm attracted attention. Possibly I was indiscreet in demonstrating my joy in learning, growing, and just plain living.

Simmet was what most reasonable people would have called a deeply troubled city. My family was unapologetically and happily entrenched in Simmet, though. We were deeply rooted there. Four generations of my family (not inclusive of my generation) had looked past the city's poverty, and taken pride in its diversity and pleasure in its inclusiveness. Somehow, they never acknowledged the limitations or dangers of living in the inner city. They adored Simmet. I, too, considered it to be a wonderful place to call home.

I had no premonition that anything would go wrong for me there until it did.

At my elementary school, I had been insulated from the rough edges of the city. My classmates had known each other nearly forever, and they were decent kids who were on an accelerated educational path. At Simmet's central junior high school, my classmates and I were scattered. I was put into a division populated by children whose life circumstances would have been impossible for me to imagine.

These were tough kids. I didn't know how they lived, why they behaved as they did, or what the rules of their society were. Also, I didn't know what I didn't know. Certainly, I wasn't equipped to handle these children. I wouldn't have had the first clue about how to fit in or what they expected of me.

Within days, I became a target for three girls in my division who seemed to be tight friends with each other. Their vitriol caught me by surprise, because I had no idea what they were responding to. As far as I knew, I hadn't done anything to provoke them. We had never had an argument or exchanged cross words.

It seemed as though they had just taken an instant dislike to me. They verbally harassed me on a continual basis in front of all the other children and any adults who might have been around. The trio had a leader who had initiated the bullying, but the other two girls willingly joined in.

They recruited others, too. Soon, nearly all of our class-mates had joined them. I had begun to make friends, but these three girls seemed to be gaining in popularity and power every moment of every day. Most of the other individuals in the class found it most expedient to ditch me and go over to the mean girls' side. Some held out for a little while, but most of them eventually succumbed.

The children seemed to be entertaining themselves at my expense. It actually looked as if they were having fun. But it was mean-spirited, and their activities all seemed to revolve around ridiculing and excluding me.

Teachers who might have intervened chose not to do so. The adults made themselves so scarce that, perhaps, they did not have much of an opportunity to see or hear what was hap-pening as things progressed.

Apparently, the children wanted to see how far they could push the boundaries and how much punishment I would take. Passive by nature, I waited for them to stop. It seemed to me they would have to move on eventually. What they were do-ing to me made no sense. They couldn't keep it up indefinitely.

Even if they didn't snap out of it, someone would save me. I wasn't equipped to make these children stop bullying me, but somebody else would. They would just have to do something.

Except that none of the adults around me were willing to get involved. Most of the teachers opted out completely. They would take attendance at the beginning of each class, leave the room, and return only in time to dismiss the children.

A handful of relatively stalwart teachers did not leave the classroom. They sat at their desks, pushing papers around —

watching the uncontrolled kids metaphorically bounce off the walls — and they looked as beleaguered as I felt.

Some of that small minority of teachers occasionally attempted to conduct classes during my junior high school experience. There were a few desultory mathematical reviews of addition and subtraction, phone-it-in social studies lessons, and lectures from a science teacher about rocks. An English class teacher based some bewilderingly insipid lessons on the original "Willy Wonka and the Chocolate Factory" movie that had been released about half a dozen years previously. If the teacher was aware that the movie had been based on a classic children's book, she never mentioned it to the class. Otherwise, teachers mostly were absent, otherwise occupied, or too distracted by something — perhaps their own fear of the students — to teach.

The lack of consistent, challenging educational activities at school left a vacuum. The three mean girls, who had gained positions of authority among their peers, rushed in to fill that gap. Their recruits ignored the teachers and took their orders from the girls who were actually in charge of the class.

It was a real-life version of "Lord of the Flies," and I was cast in the role of Piggy. The teachers might not have been able to save me even if they had tried. They seemed to be as frightened of the mean girls and my other classmates as I was.

I would try to escape from the monotony of intellectual boredom and the agony of verbal assaults by reading my textbooks, but when I did, the children would bust me for being "smart." They hurled that insult at me in the same tone of voice as they might have used to accuse me of having halitosis or of passing gas.

Who knows what that accusation meant? I suspect it was a combination of things, including a quirk of diction that made me sound as if I were perpetually auditioning for the role of William Shatner; my rapt, almost worshipful, attention on the rare occasions when any adult attempted to teach; and my tendency to use an above-grade-level vocabulary gleaned from reading a lot of books. Whatever "smart" meant to those children, I'm sure it had very little to do with my academic abilities. They didn't know anything about them.

Sometimes, I would try to write unobtrusively in my notebooks: poems, short stories, and even the beginnings of a novel. But I couldn't get away with that, either. Whatever I did inflamed the situation and placed me in further jeopardy. Mostly, I just tried not to breathe, make a sound, move, or even think.

Clocks' hands seemed stuck. I suffered endless bouts of headaches and stomachaches, but I never asked to see a nurse. Walking through the halls to get to the clinic seemed too risky. Tough kids were everywhere, and I felt threatened by every one of them. All I wanted was to get away from school and go home where I would be safe.

The name calling, mocking, and ostracism were relentless. I had no reprieve. If it was the intention of those three girls and their tribe to break me, they pretty much succeeded. My self-esteem and optimism had been shattered.

Also, I missed learning which had always been at the core of my joy. Educationally, I was losing far more than I was gaining. Neglect by my teachers combined by censure from my classmates had effectively shut down my ability to think.

Ostensibly, I was verbally attacked because of my academic inclinations, so I acquired a tremendous sense of guilt about wanting to learn. To me, pursuing an education seemed as indefensible as compulsive gambling, public intoxication, or substance abuse. It was an insupportable vice.

While I would never give it up, studying became my secret. For the remainder of my academic life — even when I took adult education classes — I would never feel entitled to participate in a class discussion or ask a question. I could never casually look at a graded paper a teacher had handed back to me, discuss my test results, or make plans to study with anyone. Seventh grade put an end to my life as an unabashed student, and I never got that back again.

The following school year, the students were reassembled into new divisions. One of the three mean girls — the leader, as it happened — ended up in my group again, but the other two did not.

Alone, the remaining mean girl seemed to back off just a bit. She still bullied me, but her enthusiasm for the sport seemed to have waned now that her friends had been replaced by strangers. I had a sense that I might be able to ignore her now, if I were lucky, and even find some friends in the mix.

Things appeared to have stabilized enough so that I regained a bit of hope. Maybe I could make a fresh start. Few of the faces around me looked familiar, and the new people had not yet judged me. I let myself believe that things might be better.

The most charismatic young boy in my class quickly caught my attention. To me, he resembled Peter Tork, my favorite member of the old Monkees musical band. I'd grown up sharing a bedroom with my two sisters, and Monkees' posters had hung on the wall for years. Pete was my pick. He had it all over Davy Jones, in my opinion. At twelve years old, I still preferred the Nordic look.

The Peter Tork lookalike was cute enough so that he probably caught everyone's attention, but I was aware only of the current that seemed to flow between us. Artlessly, I began to steal peeks at him. The first few times that I caught him grinning back, I was pleased that he was smiling at me. If I'd had more confidence in myself, I would have made a friendly overture toward him. As it was, I had to wait for him to start a conversation.

That never happened. Now that I had made his radar, he had something else in mind: shaming me. His insults and catcalls especially hurt, because I blamed myself for eliciting them. I had looked at him, and I even had hoped he would look back at me. Until then, I had thought that I was as entitled as any other pre-teen to modestly flirt with a peer. Now I knew better.

He picked up where the three mean girls had left off. Every minute of every school day provided him with another opportunity to let me know how unworthy I was and everything that was wrong about me. He wasn't content to hurt me on his own, either. With his popularity, he was able to enlist the participation of just about everyone else in the class. Things spun out of control and blew past all reasonable limits. Because my self-esteem and social skills had already been bludgeoned by my experiences with bullying the year before, I was an even easier target than I had been.

The verbal assaults were nearly constant, and they were torturous. Now the burgeoning young woman in me had also been skewered.

At about the same time, one of the original triumvirate of mean girls, who was now in another class, apparently smelled blood. Between classes, she and her new classmates regularly took turns shoving me down corridors and pushing me down steep flights of stairs.

The way it typically worked was this. A child would shove me, and I would lose my balance and miss a step or two. Then, I would just about regain my equilibrium, and another child would push me. I would miss a few more steps. A third child would push me. The game, from their point of view, was to see how few shoves it would take to make me fall down an entire flight of stairs.

There were two flights of stairs, if I remember correctly. There might have been three. That detail, I have blocked. Each of the staircases consisted of about twenty steps.

If the children had a goal in mind, only they knew what it was. Were they trying to break my limbs, sever my spinal cord, send me to a hospital, or put me in a wheelchair? Was it their hope that they could kill me? What were they trying to accomplish, and why? I never found out.

All I could do was to hold onto the banister as tightly as possible, but that was never good enough. I would fall ... and fall ... and fall. If you've ever experienced the sensation of losing your balance and endlessly falling in your nightmares (or, heaven forbid, in real life), then you know how it felt.

It was only a matter of time before I was seriously injured or worse. Sooner or later, I wouldn't be able to get back up again. What should I do? Think, Stacey. Think.

I would delay taking the stairs for as long as I could, but my torturers would wait for me. If I prolonged this, I could be late for class, and that was against the rules.

There were two ways down from the classroom where I started out: two sets of staircases, one at each end of the hall. But one flight of stairs was supposed to be used only to go downstairs. The other set of stairs could be used only to go upstairs.

Once, desperate to protect myself in the only way that came to mind, I committed an act of insubordination. I tried to go down the wrong staircase. But a teacher caught me and sent me to the other end of the hall to go downstairs properly. I followed his directions and, naturally, I was assaulted by the waiting children.

A core group of approximately eight students, mostly girls, pushed me. I knew a few of their names — mostly, because I heard them calling to each other. I'd never had any contact with them, except their ringleader, before. We didn't know each other. Between ten and twenty additional students — some from the ringleader's class, and some from my division — egged them on.

This happened on a daily basis, in full view of the teachers who were assigned to patrol the halls and stairways between classes. Some of them might have seen something, at some time. They might even have seen everything, all of the time.

But what they didn't admit to seeing, they didn't have to deal with. So, essentially, no adult saw. No adult heard.

No adult was willing to get trapped into knowing.

I can remember how my younger self felt, and I can understand why she did so little to help herself. She was terrified and immobilized by panic, horror, self-loathing, and shame.

Surely, if someone tried to assault me now, I would use my loudest possible voice to tell them to stop and to attract as much attention as I could. I would call for intervention from law enforcement, if I had access to a cell phone. I'd vocally and physically fight as hard as I could to survive.

But raising your voice in school wasn't allowed. It never occurred to me that, under the circumstances, I had a right to scream. Putting my hands on anyone in anger — even for the purposes of self-defense — was unimaginable to me. In all of my life, I had never been anything but a well-behaved child and a model student. I had been trained to fit in and to go along quietly.

What was happening to me was so outside of my experience that I couldn't begin to understand it or figure out how to disengage from the drama. Mentally, physically, emotionally, and spiritually, I was devastated. I couldn't take a single breath, utter a simple sound, or move a muscle at any time during the school day without fear.

This wasn't something I could leave inside the classroom. I brought the realities of bullying home with me after school, and I kept it with me on weekends and during days off. It stayed with me always.

The trauma was constant. It was relentless, and it overshadowed everything. There was no more normality left in my world except with my family.

My parents had always been so proud of all of their children. I couldn't tell them that I was an outcast, or that my life was in danger, at school.

My abusers had warned me that, if I ever told anyone, they would kill me. They were already hurting me so badly that I couldn't handle any more pain. I couldn't tell my parents or any other adult in my extended family, because I couldn't risk making things worse.

It seemed everyone in the school community was invested in keeping my torture a secret, and I was complicit. Of course, I fantasized about asking an adult to intervene. But I was too afraid of the consequences, and that suited everyone just fine. Remaining silent, and holding in all the pain, was the only plan I could execute.

When I finally had the opportunity to extricate myself from the situation — however bizarre and unpromising that opportunity seemed — I grabbed it.

My escape route represented the only possibility to get away from my abusers. After I'd finished the eighth grade, I left the local public school system, and I entered a parochial high school.

In other words, I ran away. That was in June 1977. The ending was abrupt and cataclysmic, and you'll hear a few of the details later on in my story.

In high school, I was left to heal, or at least to compose myself and move on, as best as I could. The parochial high school was a few miles, but a world away, from home.

Most of my classmates there had attended Catholic schools since kindergarten. My background was nothing like theirs, and the students understandably wanted to know why I was there. It was a fair question, but it was one that I could not answer. The truth was just too terrible, and embarrassing, to share.

They say that you can run, but you can't hide. That's only partly true. I actually *could* hide. And I did just that, for most of my adult life.

I hid from the truth that my junior high school years had been ravaged by bullying, and that those nightmarish experiences had informed so many of the choices I'd subsequently made. It seemed to me that pretending the bullying had never happened was the only reasonable way to proceed.

So I denied the pain of my childhood bullying. I buried it deep inside where, I believed, it would do the least amount of harm. And I successfully hid the truth until two events occurred, many years apart.

The Day of the Funeral

The first occurrence was a chance sighting at the funeral of my great-aunt Frances who passed away in May 1997.

My nuclear family, which had arrived early, paid our respects to Aunt Frances' closest relatives. Then we sat together in a middle pew of the funeral parlor and waited for the service to begin.

Other people walked in, and most of them stopped at the front of the room to pay their respects to the bereaved. We could see them from where we sat.

A nondescript woman entered and stopped to talk to my Aunt Frances' daughter-in-law. I barely noticed this person, but my older sisters apparently found something worth putting their heads together and whispering about.

I was five years younger than the sister who was closest to me in age and eight years younger than the oldest. Those were big age differences.

But only three years separated the two of them. They had much in common that I didn't share, and it wasn't unusual for the two of them to buzz about things that didn't concern me. I paid no attention to their conversation.

At one point, my oldest sister, Bonnie, leaned over to me and pointed out the woman who was talking to Aunt Frances' daughter-in-law. She whispered to me, "Is that Ms. Marino? We think it is, but we're not sure. You've seen her more recently than we have." ("Marino" is a pseudonym.)

Indeed, I had seen her more recently, but almost two decades had elapsed since then. Ms. Marino had been a guidance counselor at my junior high school.

To me, she was emblematic of everything the administrative members of my school had done wrong. I'd always felt she was the person who had let me down the most. I held a lot of people — including myself — accountable for what went wrong, but I reserved most of the blame for her. Unspoken and unaddressed, my fury at her had festered and grown for nearly twenty years.

My mother had initiated a meeting with Ms. Marino as my eighth grade year drew to a close. Like so many children who were bullied back then, I hadn't told my parents about the abuse I was experiencing. But, one day, mom had figured out for herself that something had gone terribly awry.

I had told her that I wasn't going on a class field trip that had been scheduled for that day because I was sick. Therefore, she expected me to be home in the morning when she called me from work to check on me. I didn't answer, because I wasn't there.

This was many years before cell phones were commonplace. If someone phoned you, and you weren't sitting by the landline, then you couldn't answer the call.

At the last minute, I had decided to go on the field trip. It had taken all the courage I'd had, given the fact that my classmates had assured me that they would kill me as soon as we left the school's property. I believed they would try, but I'd gone, anyway. It was wrong to take a day off school if you weren't sick.

Mom's instincts brought her home as quickly as possible to locate her missing daughter. When she didn't find me or even see a note from me, she called the school in a panic. The school's secretary transferred mom to the guidance counselor's office. Ms. Marino picked up the phone and agreed to meet with mom right away.

Ms. Marino must have felt cornered, because she spilled it all — or, at least, the parts of it that she knew. She admitted to my mother that I had been targeted by bullies almost since I had set foot in the junior high school. Everyone at the school, according to Ms. Marino, had known about the hell I was going through.

Mom was too shocked to ask the right questions. For example, she didn't ask Ms. Marino why she, and her colleagues, had failed to notify my parents or done anything to help me.

Mom listened as Ms. Marino trotted out the tired old accusation that I was much too smart for my environment. (Where did Ms. Marino even get that? When had any teacher at that school ever bothered to find out what I might be capable of learning?) The public school system, Ms. Marino concluded, couldn't accommodate my educational needs. It also couldn't guarantee my safety, given the trouble I was having.

Therefore, I couldn't go to Simmet High School. I had to go somewhere else.

Ms. Marino directed my mother to send me to a Catholic high school in the area. She said that was the only place that might be able to handle me. This woman (who had been my sisters' teacher before she was elevated to the post of guidance counselor) most likely would have been aware that my family wasn't Catholic. We were of the Jewish faith. In practice, we leaned toward orthodoxy.

Even if Ms. Marino hadn't remembered, my mother would have told her at that point in their conversation. But the guidance counselor was on a mission to shed herself of this problem in the easiest way possible, so she fixated on the plan that she most likely formulated on the spur of the moment. She would toss me overboard.

The guidance counselor provided my mother with just enough outdated information to convince her that our religion wouldn't be a problem at the Catholic high school. I wouldn't have to enroll in religion classes, she assured mom.

Anyway, if my parents wouldn't send me to this Catholic high school, that was it. Ms. Marino had no other ideas. She'd offered my mother her advice. Mom could take it or leave it.

After that meeting, my mom explained to me that we had to apply for admission to the parochial high school. She quoted Ms. Marino: "If you love your daughter, you'll send her to Saint Francis High School." (The name of the school is fictitious. Her comment, however, is not.)

My parents did, indeed, love me. It was also true that they innately trusted authority figures and would never have felt qualified to argue with one of them. So my parents allowed me to be exiled to Saint Francis High School when I was 13 years old.

Ms. Marino's "she's too smart" accusation was ironic given the academic struggles I was about to encounter in high school. Because I had been denied an education for the two years I had spent in junior high school — and had been attacked every time I tried to open up a book or to lift a writing implement — I had to begin the ninth grade with something less than a sixth grade education. It would take me at least a year to catch up to my grade level, and I couldn't tell a single soul why. That meant I couldn't ask any of my teachers for help. I studied and struggled all alone, in the closet.

Although I thirsted for knowledge, it was unclear what I could do about it. Everything that seemed to come naturally to my classmates — listening to lectures, taking notes, prioritizing words in textbooks, and retrieving memorized information during exams — had become as alien to me as the crucifixes that hung on the walls of every enclosed space around me.

As a puzzled history teacher explained to my parents during the first PTA meeting, "She seems bright enough. It's just that she doesn't *know* anything." Motivation bordering on obsession and excruciatingly hard work finally enabled me to fill in enough of those academic gaps so that I could move forward with my peers. But Ms. Marino's accusation that I was "too smart" to fit in with ordinary students had been just plain nonsense.

And Ms. Marino was incorrect about something else, too. Saint Francis High School *did* require all students to enroll in theology classes throughout my time there. A private school such as Saint Francis High School had the right to make the rules, and I had the obligation to follow them if I wanted to stay.

Attending Saint Francis High School would turn out to be a bizarre experience for me. I would spend four years as a semi-permanent guest, rather than an actual member of the student body. The school community, by and large, treated me as an honored guest — a visiting dignitary, of sorts. However, as gracious, warm, and nurturing as the people at Saint Francis High School were, I knew that I had no right to be there. I was completely dependent on the kindness of strangers.

Circumstances had cast me as the love child of Kato Kaelin and Blanche DuBois. Who would choose that role?

Don't get me wrong. It was a pretty soft landing. The Saint Francis High School community members, for the most part, went out of their way to make me feel welcome and wanted. Exceptions were notable but, of course, understandable.

No one ever told me that my presence was an imposition, but they didn't have to. I could see for myself that, despite the kindness and affection nearly everyone showered on me, I was a nuisance.

What were they supposed to do with the Jewish kid during masses? Where was she supposed to hide her forehead on Ash Wednesday? Who would volunteer to tutor the Jewish girl so that she could get sophomore-level credit for a religion course without having to study the sacraments with the rest of her class? How were teachers and students supposed to deliver such lines as, "We, as Christians..." or "The Christian thing to do is..." when they would be excluding someone who was sitting in the room?

The Saint Francis High School community created new rules, and a new lexicon, to accommodate my needs. That was wonderful of them, and it may well have saved my life ... but it wasn't fair to them or to me.

This was a Catholic school, and it was for Catholic students. I didn't come close to qualifying. Although my parents paid my tuition, as all the other parents did, I felt like a charity case. Always, I felt like a freak.

All of that was on Ms. Marino's head. She had made the initial phone call to the parochial high school's admissions office to have an application rushed to my home, and she'd made another call to have the entrance exam requirement waived, since it was too late for me to take the test.

The guidance counselor had orchestrated a fast-as-lightning campaign to have several of my junior high school teachers — who, themselves, had known what I was going through and had ignored my predicament — write the necessary letters of recommendation.

Ms. Marino had done everything except buy me a school uniform and get me a bus schedule so that I could attend Saint Francis High School's freshman orientation. For me, it was an insane ending to a prolonged nightmare, and I blamed the guidance counselor who had so casually made it happen.

If Ms. Marino ever felt remorse or guilt about failing to intervene while I was her responsibility, or for coming up with a crazy way to rid herself and her school system of the responsibility of dealing with me, I never found out about it. If she ever made any inquiries to find out whether I was faring well enough at Saint Francis High School or needed to find an alternative, I never heard about that, either.

I had never heard anything from Ms. Marino after the day she'd essentially expelled me from the Simmet school system. And, now, my sister was articulating her name: "Is that Ms. Marino?"

At my Aunt Frances' funeral, I looked at the person who might or might not have been Ms. Marino. It had been so long since I'd seen her, and my facial recognition skills were exceptionally poor. But, finally, the woman's face came into focus for me. I positively identified her.

"Yes," I told my sister. "That is Ms. Marino." The funeral service began.

The memories involving Ms. Marino and all that she represented nearly engulfed me during the service. I pushed them away.

Afterwards, my sister, Bonnie, and I got into her car to drive to the *shiva* house. After she'd started the engine, and we were no longer able to make eye contact, Bonnie said, "I wasn't exactly thrilled to see Ms. Marino, either. She wasn't one of my favorite teachers. But you're really upset. What's going on? Talk to me."

I'm typically a fairly self-contained person, and I do not routinely express anger, let alone primal rage. So what happened next surprised me and must have terrified my sister, who had to drive. I started to scream, full voice, and I couldn't stop until I'd exhausted myself.

Bonnie was my best friend, but I had never told her about my experiences in junior high school. She may have heard bits and pieces of the story, but she didn't hear any of them from me. All Bonnie ever heard from me, personally, were those screams of rage, horror, grief, and pain.

By the time Bonnie and I had arrived at the *shiva* house, I was gutted. We went inside. Because the home was filled with people who were grieving, my irregular breathing and lack of composure probably seemed reasonable. On top of everything else, obviously, I mourned the loss of my great-aunt Frances.

I hid behind Bonnie, as I did in so many social situations in those days, and I let her handle all of the necessary conversations with our relatives. Eventually, I calmed down, and I got through the condolence call. Bonnie and I never talked about what had happened in her car afterwards.

But during that car ride to the *shiva* house, I'd let just a little bit of my rage escape. Then the lid snapped shut on my emotions, and it didn't crack open again until January of 2010.

The Loss of Phoebe Prince

January 2010 was when I heard the news that a 15-year-old named Phoebe Prince had committed suicide. Phoebe, who had lived in South Hadley, Massachusetts, had been bullied to death.

Her story unfolded over the next few days and weeks. New details kept emerging.

Phoebe had moved to Massachusetts from Ireland. She'd innocently made some missteps socially for which she was ostracized, and worse, by her classmates. She had come home from school on that final day and ended her pain in the only way available to her. She had used a rope.

I cried for Phoebe and about how she'd been hurt. My heart broke because of how her story had ended.

She could have been my daughter. In fact, she could have been a younger version of *me*. I wanted to embrace Phoebe, console her, and fix things for her. I mourned for her as though she were a friend.

Phoebe hadn't deserved this, because she had found the courage to do what I hadn't. She had broken the code of silence that surrounded bullying. Phoebe had told her mother that she was being tormented, and her mother apparently asked school administrators for help more than once.

Apparently, Phoebe, herself, had also repeatedly asked teachers and school administrators to intervene on her behalf. They rarely did.

Ultimately, Phoebe lost all hope, and then she died.

I knew the strength it had taken for Phoebe to break the silence that protects bullies. When I was in junior high school and in Phoebe's position, I knew that confiding in an adult was the right thing to do, too.

I believed, with all of my being, that if I'd been able to reach out to an adult, help would have been forthcoming. That's what adults did. They helped children. Therefore, I'd always blamed myself for what happened to me. I felt that I had failed myself. Because I was incapable and unwilling to ask for help, I had caused my own grief.

But Phoebe had done what I couldn't. She had vocalized how she was feeling. Phoebe had talked about the harassment she was experiencing. She had put her faith in adults, and when that plan didn't work, she believed nothing would.

Phoebe's death changed everything for me. It finally allowed me to let myself off the hook and stop blaming myself. It provided me with the first evidence that maybe I had made an adaptive choice in keeping silent.

If I'd tried and failed to solve my problem by reaching out to adults, the way that Phoebe had, then I might have made the same final choice as she did. My story might have had the same ending as hers.

My situation had never been in my control. I hadn't created it, and I couldn't necessarily have stopped it, either.

My weakness or cowardice had not been the problem. Bullying had been the issue. I could share in the responsibility for what went wrong, but I couldn't accept all of it. The fault wasn't completely mine.

Phoebe's death was a personal tragedy for me, but it was also a revelation. It allowed me to forgive myself.

It also enraged me. Phoebe should have been enjoying every moment of her teenage years and looking forward to what came next. Instead, she was gone, and the teenagers who had tortured her had, at the end of court proceedings, walked away with probation and community service.

The South Hadley High School administrators and teachers had avoided all legal responsibility. They didn't even have to take a day off work, as far as I could tell.

There was no justice for Phoebe Prince or her family. And there was no comfort for me, either.

Once again, the lid that sealed my emotions popped open and, this time, it stayed that way.

This time, my screaming didn't take place inside of a moving vehicle with only my sister as a witness. The expression of my grief had no container and no limits.

I still wasn't able to articulate the full scope of my reaction, but I spoke to everyone who would listen about the horror of Phoebe's life and death. Nearly everyone I talked with felt terrible about the story, but only up to a certain point. For most of them, Phoebe's death was just another news story, and it got old quickly.

Several people thought my response was excessive, and some of them expressed their confusion about why I was getting so worked up about the death of someone I didn't know. When they pressed me to explain why I was reacting so emotionally, I couldn't tell them the details.

But I was able to say the phrase: "I was bullied, too." Phoebe's tragedy gave me permission to divulge that information after 35 years.

I wanted to feel relieved and unburdened. Now that my big secret was out, I wanted the trauma to magically be resolved.

40 · STACEY J. MILLER

But, somehow, things didn't work out that way. I still hadn't faced the trauma of my childhood bullying, and the issue was coming to the forefront in a big way.

CHAPTER FOUR

A NEW PERCEPTION OF BULLYING

About the time of Phoebe Prince's suicide, there were other deaths that were in the news. Phoebe wasn't the first young person to die because of bullying at school, and she wasn't the last.

Bullying at school was seemed to be all over the media. It was suddenly a hot topic, and it became unavoidable.

I became aware that some schools finally were taking a stand. They most likely weren't inventing anti-bullying policies — those paper plans had been around for a while — but they were taking those policies more seriously.

Perhaps Phoebe's death touched other hearts, as it had mine, and school administrators finally started to feel they ought to take responsibility for protecting their students from the bullying that was taking place within the school (and, in the case of cyber bullying, beyond its physical space).

Or, as the cynic in me suggests, maybe school administrators were scared in the wake of all the visibility that Phoebe's story received. They likely realized that things could have

42 · STACEY J. MILLER

turned out differently, and that Phoebe's death could have cost the South Hadley school district all of the money it had. Some of South Hadley's citizens could have gone to jail. They had narrowly escaped paying a financial penalty for causing the death of one of their students. If these events had happened in South Hadley, they could happen anywhere. So, in the spirit of protecting themselves, school administrators felt they needed to take action.

Regardless of why it happened, the fact that school systems began to convey the right messages about bullying represented progress.

School districts now have strategies in place for dealing with bullying and, theoretically, every adult and child knows what to do if something seems amiss at school. Zero-tolerance policies exist. School resource officers and liaison officers are in place, in part, to help keep kids safe.

Maybe some of those plans do discourage, or even prevent, bullying. As time goes on, maybe schools will get increasingly better at this. Someday, rampant bullying in schools might be just an unpleasant footnote in the history of education.

For now, though, bullying still happens, and when it does, neither students nor adults are reliably prosecuted or convicted for the damage they've created or allowed. At the time of this writing, it's still entirely up to the people who are bullied to figure out how to get themselves to the other side of the experience and deal with the aftermath.

No school district, of which I'm aware, has a plan in place to counsel adults who were targeted by bullies and who are still affected by the fallout. The long-term consequences of bullying still go unaddressed.

If adults want to gain mastery over the residual effects of childhood bullying, we have to do it ourselves.

Defining Bullying

Childhood bullying is a form of child abuse. It's what happens when stronger kids brutalize weaker kids and everyone else looks the other way.

We all know bullying when we experience it, even though it may take different forms. Attacks may be verbal or physical, or both. They can escalate from minor to life ending.

Predators can issue threats. They can withhold the two things their targets need the most: a sense of belonging and a feeling of safety.

Every child who experiences bullying responds to it individually. Some children laugh at bullies and walk away from the experience, whole and unscathed.

Other children feel powerless, ashamed, and devastated by the bullying. They may constantly expect abuse, and they may always be defensive and anxious.

These children may grow into adults who experience post traumatic stress disorder, or at least a variation of it. In the book that I mentioned earlier, *Bullying Scars*, author Ellen Walser deLara, PhD, MSW differentiates PTSD from what she calls adult post-bullying syndrome (APBS).

PTSD, according to Dr. deLara, provides no benefits to offset the damage it causes. On the other hand, as hurtful as APBS is, it sometimes can have positive effects. It can create empathy and compassion, and it can also motivate people to succeed.

Now that we have a label for APBS, and we have a decent description of what happens to adults who have experienced childhood bullying, we have a starting point. The bullying we experienced in the past has become mentionable, and we have the vocabulary to talk about it. We can move forward.

CHAPTER FIVE

HEALING FROM THE PAST

Why do we need a self-help book about recovering from childhood bullying? If you have to ask the question, then consider yourself lucky. You most likely don't need such a book.

You might have been bullied as a child and handled it as well as Egypt Ufele, a 10-year-old girl who designed a successful line of plus-size clothing called Chubbi Line after her peers tormented her because of her body's shape. Her fashion venture became so successful (her clothing line was eventually carried by Walmart) that she could have chosen to jeer at the children who bullied her and the adults who allowed it — but she didn't waste her energy doing that. Instead, she chose to mentor children around the world and become an ambassador of peace.

Maybe, like Egypt, you were one of those resilient children who were able to bounce back from bullying and carry on with a future that was unmarred — and perhaps even enhanced — by the experience. Your wounds might have healed without leaving scars.

The experience of enduring bullying might have strengthened you and made you more compassionate. It might have turned you into an advocate for people whose pain has been ignored or trivialized by others. You might have become a better, gentler person because of it while bearing none of the signs of PTSD. In fact, maybe the people who know you would never believe you were once a target of bullies.

We're all wired differently.

Other people who endured bullying in their childhoods may not be as fortunate. They might have incurred more, or a different type of, damage, or they just might not have been as well equipped to heal from the trauma. For some people, the residual negative effects of childhood bullying may still be evident. They may be good, caring individuals who have not healed.

For those who want to create closure and find peace, once and for all, there is good news. There is a way to move beyond the memories and get a handle on the pain, although it may require some counter-intuitive reasoning and difficult choices.

Healing may mean revisiting the past, in one way or another. Don't expect to wear white gloves while you dig in the dirt of that garden. Exercise more caution than you think you must, because you could be unearthing a world of hurt, anger, sadness, loneliness, and betrayal.

Remember to take care of yourself. Any other stressors that exist in your life can combine with your looking back and trigger mental health difficulties. Pay attention to your eating, sleeping, exercise, work, and social habits. If you notice any changes, reach out for help. Do whatever is necessary to stay healthy.

You may benefit from the support of a qualified mental health professional or, at least, someone in whom you can confide.

Respect the individuality of your journey. Everyone handles the effects of bullying differently.

Some people can't face one more moment of the suffering, and they see no hope of a positive ending. They may take their own lives.

Others direct their rage outward. They may turn their schools into shooting galleries and violently pursue their oppressors.

Still others keep the hurt inside where it festers.

Many people who experience childhood trauma suffer long-term physical and mental health consequences that extend into adulthood. These may include substance abuse, depression, and an increased risk of heart attack, stroke, coronary disease, and chronic pain.

However, most people who experience the trauma of childhood bullying survive. We grow up. We move on.

Inevitably, we mature. Our life experiences provide us with a broader context in which to place the experiences of our childhood.

But that doesn't mean the trauma disappears. We don't forget just because we're older and wiser, and the bruises may have faded.

Growing older isn't the same thing as healing. Aging may only provide us with the time and skills to bury the hurt deeply enough so that we never to know when, or how, it will surface.

Someone may innocently utter a word or phrase that triggers a flashback. Insults, intimidation, unkindness, disrespect, rejection, or even an argument with a loved one can catapult us right back to that dark place in our childhood.

Things happen. Another school year begins. Bullying Prevention Month fills the media. News outlets report stories about school-related bullying, violence, suicide, and homicide.

In many ways, bullying has grown even worse over the years. No longer is it limited to taunting and exclusion at school and threats (or the manifestation) of fighting beyond the classroom. It now involves online harassment and violence that can involve rape, knives, bombs, and guns. With 24/7/365 access to news, it's possible to find at last a few bullying-related stories each week.

The events that reopen our wounds do not have to relate directly to school bullying, either. Trauma is trauma. It's all the same, regardless of the details.

When we hear about children screaming as they're ripped out of their parents' arms at the U.S. border; when we discover that approximately sixty women were likely drugged and raped by a formerly beloved comedian/actor; when someone who is accused of sexually assaulting a 15-year-old and others is appointed as a U.S. Supreme Court justice; when we learn that anyone is suffering an injustice or that anyone has gotten away with committing one ... we may find ourselves being torn apart again.

Every person's pain, when we hear about it, may trigger our own. One moment, we're here, and the next, we're not. We're back where it all began.

That can happen to you until you determine that you have given up enough of your present-day moments to unresolved pain and find a way to heal. That is the reason you're reading a book about getting past childhood bullying.

The world is so much smaller now than it once was. Social media has exponentially increased the likelihood that you'll run into people who were part of your past. Although social networking can be an asset in the recovery process (more about that later), it can also trigger memories from which you haven't healed.

A former antagonist may send you a friend request via a social network, and that can send you into a tailspin. An overture may come from a member of the bully's inner social circle, or someone who was there at the time and saw everything. Simply knowing that someone from the past may find your contact information online and try to connect with you can be disturbing.

So leaving the scene of your childhood does not necessarily provide lasting peace. The possibility of being ambushed is always there. The past can encroach upon the present at any time, and you can reasonably expect it to happen when you're least equipped to deal with it. Childhood bullying is a landmine that tends to stay buried.

The path I've found to healing is through facing the past. You may find that works for you, too. Make peace with the abusers and events of the past, and their power over you will diminish.

Unfortunately, you can't lift up a rock and expect to find healing conveniently hiding beneath it. You won't stumble upon peace from the trauma of childhood bullying by accident.

The work is arduous, and it involves choosing the direction that is right for you. What's best for you today may be different from what will work best at another time.

So choose your path in accordance with your current needs, but know that you can always change your mind. You can begin by staying squarely in your comfort zone. Later on, you can venture outside of that space, one step at a time.

The bigger the risks, the greater the potential rewards ... but you may reap all the benefits you need by taking the smallest steps possible, at your own pace.

CHAPTER SIX

THE REASONS FOR SILENCE

If you have kept silent, then your secret might have festered inside of you all these years. In that case, you may decide it's time to change that strategy and tell your story. You may also choose to share it.

The only expert on the bullying you experienced is you. That means you have something worthwhile to say. Your story of survival may inspire others who are not sure they can, or even want to, outlive the problem of bullying.

Bullies torture. That's what they do. They exploit the disparity in power between themselves and their targets, and they enjoy causing pain.

They are sadists. They are button pushers. They take pleasure in what they do.

In a space ruled primarily by children, there are few limitations to the harm bullies can inflict. There are no boundaries. There is no empathy. There is no mercy.

For those who are targeted by bullies, the experience can be devastating. They can suffer alone with few options, little reprieve, and no escape.

Bullying at school has long been a dirty secret. People know it happens. But people rarely acknowledge its gravity or the lasting effects it can have on those who are targeted. Therefore, people who experience bullying at school often suffer in silence. Then, as adults, they continue to keep the secret.

Children who are targeted by bullies may be threatened with retribution if they tell anyone their secret. Although they already are suffering, they may believe things can get even worse. They may imagine the forms the bullies' revenge could take and decide not to risk it.

They may also blame themselves. Along with feeling ashamed that they are being tortured by their peers, they may also feel guilty. They may believe that, somehow, they did something to deserve it.

Children who are overwhelmed by shame can't face their parents and other family members with the truth. They may believe their parents would be shattered by the problem, or that they would hand it over to school administrators — and that would only make things worse.

Home may be children's only sanctuary, and they may not want to risk the safety of that space by bringing the brutality of bullying into it.

Also, bullying happens out in the open. It isn't hidden at school.

Teachers, paraprofessionals, coaches, and administrators — and even librarians, school bus drivers, nurses, and custodians — usually know about the bullying, because it happens in full view of them. Any adult at, or associated with, the school who does not see and hear the bullying has invested a lot of energy in neither seeing nor hearing. That adult does not want to know.

Teachers, coaches, administrators, and other adults who are involved with children at school may assume everyone will live through the experience of bullying without their intervention. Maybe it will even toughen up the children who are targeted. In any case, children should handle it themselves. They expect them to ignore it, if that's possible, or fight back, if it's necessary. But they don't want to know the specifics of what is going on. They do not want the burden of having to deal with the problem.

Bullying, even when it leads to physical assault, is rarely seen as a crime. People see it as a necessary evil. Even kids may believe their suffering is something they should be able to endure. Few children would willingly approach a principal, teacher, or law enforcement official if they are in trouble.

Later on, when children who are bullied become adults, they have already been conditioned to keep silent about their negative childhood experiences. Adults are always encouraged to be positive and upbeat. No one wants to be around a Debbie Downer or listen to what she might have endured when she was a child. Adults all have their own baggage, and few would want to hear about what anyone else has suffered.

So adults maintain their habit of keeping quiet about their past. They bury it below layers of defenses. If necessary, they lie to hide gaps in the narratives of their lives. They hope that, someday, they will forget. Maybe, if they keep silent about the past, it will just go away.

They never resolve the memories that haunt them. They never find peace, and they never experience closure.

54 · STACEY J. MILLER

Keeping the secret and locking all of that hurt inside can take far more energy than coming clean. Telling the story can be a first step toward healing, once and for all.

CHAPTER SEVEN

TELLING YOUR STORY, PART 1

Society has demanded silence, or outright denial, about the experience of bullying until recently. You probably haven't shouted your personal experiences with it from the mountaintops, either.

You may never have told anyone about the horrors you suffered at the hands of childhood bullies.

If you can tell your story, then you can face the truth about what happened to you. That will let you start processing those memories and prepare you to move on.

Otherwise, you may perpetually replay the worst parts of your childhood experiences as if they were the sounds of a scratched vinyl record. Every time you replay the event, you create memories of remembering, and those memories will be fresh and raw. The terrible things you experienced in your childhood will always seem to be happening in the present.

They will never recede into the back of your mind where they belong. The bad memories will take up permanent, rent-free residence in your head. They will occupy space that you could put to far better use in storing memories that elicit contentment, pride, and hope.

If you maintain the secret of what happened to you in your childhood, then you may have to live with the consequences of those events forever. If you deal with your memories, once and for all, you can get past them.

Your story is yours to tell — your way, and on your timetable. Telling that story is a way to take back your power.

Those who led you to believe that bullying happened to everyone, and you just had to accept it, were wrong.

The experiences you suffered at the hands of bullies should not have been a dirty little secret. Keeping silent about what happened is not your obligation, and protecting the perpetrators by keeping quiet is not your responsibility.

Insulating yourself from the shame and pain you felt when you were living through the events is no longer your mandate. Everything has changed.

Society now understands that bullying has consequences. You have been part of the conspiracy of silence long enough. While you cannot erase the past, you can begin to heal from your experiences by acknowledging them.

Telling your story provides you with an opportunity to reframe the events so that you can better understand, synthesize, and learn from them. You can correct the misperceptions and maladaptive beliefs you might have swallowed in your childhood. Your adult perspective can help.

It may seem impossible, after all this time has elapsed, to confront your memories of that time and place. You may believe it would be too difficult to revisit the source of your trauma.

You may think it's best to just let sleeping dogs lie. Perhaps you're right. Maybe sleeping dogs are best left alone. But that doesn't necessarily apply to sleeping monsters.

But maybe the antagonists of your childhood are no longer the monsters you imagine them to be. You may be stronger than they are now, and they may no longer hold any position of power over you. In that case, all of the choices about dealing with them would be yours.

Elements of your story have probably been looping around in your conscious or subconscious, anyway, just begging to be heard. Guiding your story into the world, and exposing it to the light, is your prerogative.

You don't have to be a professional storyteller to do it. No one is judging your efforts. This is your story. You can tell it your way.

If you tell the story to yourself, that's fine. If you choose to share it with others, that's also okay.

You may have been one of the rare children who were able to tell the story while it was unfolding. Perhaps you shared it with an adult or a peer, either willingly or unwillingly. The bullies may have been caught in the act, and the adults in your life may have found out about it. Perhaps they even witnessed it.

But they might not have successfully intervened. Perhaps, if adults heard your story or even saw it unfold, they did not provide you with the help you deserved. Maybe they ignored your story or responded to it with derision.

If your story got out there once, that's not necessarily the end of it. You can repackage the story and tell it again. This time, you can infuse your story with the wisdom and experience you've gained in the years between then and now.

As you prepare to tell your story, remember that you are not an outlier or a freak. This happened to so many of us.

In the United States, one out of every three students reports he or she was bullied at school, according to the U.S. Department of Health and Human Services. Given those statistics, you may be one of millions of former targets whose story has never been told. It may be time to change that.

Beginning Your Narrative

Tell the story as if it belongs to someone who has great worth and who truly matters. Believe that you do have a right to tell your truth.

These are your recollections, and you are their sole owner. Tell as much, or as little, of the story as you feel safe remembering.

It may be more than slightly uncomfortable. You may find yourself raging at the abuse to which you were subjected as you begin to remember the perpetrators and the enablers. The short-term result may be an abundance of grief. You may re-live the feelings of helplessness, pain, despair, and humiliation. Be prepared for the avalanche of emotions, and trust that it is better to face your feelings than to suppress or repress them. Drag the story from the basement of your consciousness into the light of your maturity and experience.

The truth is yours to tell, and the storytelling is yours to manage when you are ready. You will be in charge of gathering all of the components you may feel it's important to include.

You are the star of your own story. The other characters may vary, from one situation to another. Setting and events may differ.

But here are some categories that you may want to consider including as you think about your own story. Some may resonate with you. Others may not. But they can serve as starter ideas to help you formulate your representation of the way things happened for you.

Every story begins with its characters, and you play the leading role in this one. Your part in the story matters more than anyone else's, because this is all about you.

The Characters

The Child You Were

The child you once were is the protagonist of the story.

Perhaps the story starts before you were even born, with your parents or your ancestors. Perhaps it starts before the advent of civilization. This is your story, and you can tell it the way that you want.

Chances are, though, your story of childhood bullying started when someone — or some people — decided to take away your innocence. That may be the best place to begin.

The kids who least deserve it may be most likely to serve as bullies' targets. Maybe they are chosen by bullies because, for one reason or another, they are vulnerable. Their innocence puts a target on their backs.

Reflect on the child you were before the bullying began. You'll probably remember that you possessed traits like these: You were trusting, open, optimistic, and congenial.

Maybe you stood out because of your ethnicity, body type, accent, speech patterns, abilities, mannerisms, or style.

You certainly wanted the things every other child craves: acceptance, safety, identity, and a sense of belonging.

Why should any of these attributes or desires be punishable by abuse? And who appointed those other children your judge and jury, anyway?

Maybe you were targeted because you were similar to unspoiled bubble wrap. Most of us, at some point, have enjoyed the sensation of popping fresh, puffy cells, one at a time. Each time we crack one, we feel a small sense of satisfaction. Snap. Snap. Snap. Miss one? Try again. SNAP! Got it that time.

Once all of the bubbles have been deflated, though, the fun is gone. You don't want to play with a roll of spent bubble wrap. You have to find an intact section of bubble wrap to continue.

Similarly, some bullies wouldn't want to waste their energy harassing kids who are already broken. They want to target healthy, thriving, self-confident children so they can experience that popping sensation. It provides them a cheap sense of control and a warped sense of accomplishment. They feel the joy of making the kill.

As a child, you may have been the bubble wrap. If so, then you were full of the life force. You were infused with energy and vitality.

Then you met people who exploited that vigor and who commandeered your positive energy.

Maybe they tried to take your possessions away from you. That might have caused you embarrassment and inconvenience. Maybe you even found yourself in trouble for "losing" things for which you were responsible and which someone —

your parents or maybe the school system — had paid for and entrusted you with.

It's likely that the bully sought something beyond the items you owned or that were in your care. The bully was probably less attracted by your possessions than by the intangible things you carried with you: your self-esteem, pride, confidence, and happiness.

A bully can't pull those things out of your arms, or grab them from your desk, backpack, or locker. Instead, the bully stole the invisible attributes you had such as your equanimity. The antagonists may have sucked the joy out of your soul like an industrial strength vacuum cleaner.

Or maybe someone else had been there first.

Maybe you already had crossed paths with bullies from your neighborhood, play group, or a school you had previously attended. You might have moved as a child from a community where you encountered bullies. It's also possible that members of your own family were the first bullies you faced.

The bullies you met earlier on might have done a thorough job of teaching you how to survive abuse by keeping as silent and still as you could. They might have groomed you to be their perfect target and a good prospect for the next batch of bullies who came along.

Maybe you'd been weakened by the experience of fending off bullies, whether it was from your earliest years or during another interlude of your childhood. It's possible you experienced abuse from the moment you entered school. Every year, the situation might have escalated as you became more frightened, hurt, and scarred.

Children smell fear, and they sense insecurity and weakness. A certain type of bully will pounce on a child who seems susceptible and vulnerable. That child might have been you.

Your past experiences might have turned you into a vastly different version of the child you wished to be and, under different circumstances, could have become. Because of the abuse you experienced, you might have become defensive and withdrawn.

You might have experienced depression and anxiety that resulted in insomnia. Maybe you stopped paying close attention to your eating, grooming, or personal hygiene habits. Your sleep might have been forfeited. Academically, your progress might have slowed or even halted. Your social skills might have been stunted. Perhaps you gave up your extracurricular activities and lost interest in your hobbies.

Maybe you developed physical ailments due to stress and anxiety. Your immune system might have been compromised.

Possibly, you developed an eating disorder. Maybe you cut yourself or abused substances. Perhaps you contemplated ending your life, and maybe you came close to succeeding. Maybe you cried out for help in the only way you could, through self-harm. Possibly, nobody heard.

You might have found yourself engulfed in a cocoon of negativity, unhappiness, and toxicity that invited further sanctions from bullies. And, once one of those abusers drew blood, the others surrounded their prey and moved in for the kill.

Bullying involves isolating the targeted child. The practice of ostracizing comes from Ancient Greece where a person was voted out of society on a temporary basis.

In the case of a modern-day classroom, ostracism can be permanent. While other children are bonding and establishing lifelong friendships, you were excluded from their society. In fact, abusing you might have been the group activity that formed the infrastructure of the society.

It was devastating to the one who was excluded. That person could have been anybody, but it happened to be you.

Maybe you stood out from the crowd in some way. It's possible you had a quirky sense of humor. Maybe you were more mature, more verbal, more engaging, more animated, or more joyful ... or maybe you were just more fully *there* than some of the other kids were.

Abusers might have zeroed in on your family circumstances rather than on you. Maybe you came from a broken home, and your family didn't strike them as good enough. Conversely, maybe you came from an unusually intact home, and your family life seemed better than theirs. Maybe you just came from the wrong home.

Possibly, you weren't exactly like everyone else in the ways that mattered to the other children in your sphere. That might have made you unsatisfactory, as far as they were concerned. Maybe it made you seem threatening to them.

To put it another way, maybe you were extraordinary. You might have been spectacular.

If you were different in any way, positive or negative, that might have been enough to trigger someone's rage. You might have been held responsible for things that were completely beyond your control.

Abusers might have decided to target you for any reason, or for no reason. Well, so what?

64 · STACEY J. MILLER

You might have internalized everyone else's opinion of you and judged yourself to be partly responsible for it. If you had been normal, whatever that meant at the time, then you might not have been the target of the bullies. If you hadn't been strong and thriving, the bullies might not have been motivated to derail you. If you hadn't been hurt and wounded, the bullies might not have endeavored to destroy you.

If you'd been someone else altogether, with a different combination of personality traits and responses to other people and situations, then those who were looking for a target might have chosen someone else. Maybe you feel guilty, because you let the bullies matter so much. Perhaps you blame yourself for being overly sensitive. You may believe that you chose to yield your strength and innocence to them. Perhaps you think you could, and should, have done something to prevent, or end, the abuse.

Instead of blaming your abusers, or the adults who failed to intervene on your behalf, you may harbor a grudge against the kid you used to be. You may feel angry that you allowed yourself to be the target of bullying.

There was a vast amount of venom directed at the child you were from other people. Perhaps you internalized that rage and felt responsible for it.

You may still remember the bullies' verbal assaults against you: the taunts and the accusations they levied. It might have sounded something like this:

You were too tall (or too short); too fat (or too thin); too light-skinned (or too dark-skinned); too quiet (or too loud); too opinionated (or too complacent); too talkative (or too introverted); too stubborn (or too yielding); too smart (or too slow); too aggressive (or too passive); too poised (or too awkward); too vulgar (or too prissy); or too rich (or too poor).

Or you subscribed to the wrong religion or ethnicity, the wrong sexual orientation, or the wrong state of health. Or you listened to the wrong type of music. Or you ate the wrong food. Or you wore the wrong clothes. Or you had the wrong hobbies. Or you weren't coordinated enough or good at sports.

Or your accent was wrong; your hair was wrong; or your face was wrong.

Or something was wrong with one or more of your family members or friends.

You had no value. You were useless.

We don't want you. Go away. Evaporate. Disappear. Die.

The voices were probably as persistent as they were nasty. When you heard them enough, you might have started to believe them. Perhaps you can hear those words now as clearly as you could hear them then.

Those words helped shape the image you had of yourself back then, and they might have crushed your self esteem. But that doesn't mean they were true. The fact that you might have believed them doesn't provide them with validity.

Your abusers had all the power, and you had none. Therefore, you believed what they told you.

But their words were never intended to provide you with helpful feedback. Their words were designed to hurt you. They weren't true then, and they are no truer now than they were when you were a child.

You may have bought into the taunts that you heard and with which you were once surrounded. But you don't have to hold onto them anymore.

They came from the people who antagonized you, and you're not obligated to see them as your truth. You're not required to feel a sense of guilt or shame because of those words. You don't have to own them.

Bullies were going to label you and attack you, one way or another. There was no way to escape it. Nothing you could have said or done would have prevented it.

The specific things they said about you were beside the point. These kids were on a mission to control their environment as best as they could, any way they could. Part of their strategy was to pick on another child, and you happened to be their scapegoat.

Perhaps the bullying went beyond verbal taunts. Maybe it included threats of violence. Possibly, the abuse escalated into one or more physical assaults that may, or may not, have included a sexual component.

Whatever form the bullying took, it was abuse. You may wish you hadn't responded to it the way that you did. Maybe you cowered and showed your weakness. It is possible you returned the attack verbally or physically. Maybe you traded insults and threats with the bullies or with other classmates, and maybe you hurt the feelings of others just as they hurt yours.

Or maybe you didn't react outwardly. Instead, maybe you kept your feelings to yourself. It is possible that you walled yourself off and tried to make yourself as small as possible. Maybe you tried to become invisible.

You may criticize yourself because of the way you did, or didn't, respond. Perhaps you tell yourself that, if only you had asked for help, someone would have provided it. Maybe you should have been able to rise above the harassment and stay strong.

If you had been impervious to the bullying, maybe it would have ended. Maybe, then, the bullies would have found themselves an easier target and left you alone.

If you'd been a different person back then, maybe you wouldn't have been targeted by the bullies. Or perhaps you could have gotten the help you needed.

Another, more resilient, child might have been able to handle everything alone. Maybe that child wouldn't have needed outside intervention at all. Maybe another person could have dealt with the problem gracefully and effectively.

You could have been that other child. Perhaps you could have laughed off the bullying and, by so doing, diffused the tense situation. Maybe everyone around you would have admired you and considered you a leader, and maybe you would have made some lifelong friends in the process of saving yourself.

Sure. You also might have had memories of reading dozens of self-help books on emotional intelligence, winning friends, influencing people, making small talk, attracting positive energy, and charming strangers. And maybe you could have had all the wisdom that adult life experiences would bring, although you were a child.

But maybes don't change anything. What happened is what happened.

You weren't perfect, and you were in a horrible situation. As a child, you hadn't had time to accumulate a tool chest of coping strategies. You were not born with those skills.

At the time, you lacked perspective. You could not understand that the people around you were only a small part of a much bigger, and much more significant, universe. You hadn't had time to learn that childhood would give way to adulthood, and that the childhood bullies would probably have very little significance in your grownup world.

These abusers took up so much space in your life, and they mattered so very much. You couldn't have known that wouldn't always be the case, and that it would only be true for a relatively small period of time.

Your world was a frightening place as long as the bullies were in charge of it. They determined where you could go, how you could get there, and what you could do when you arrived. Where you couldn't go, and what you couldn't do, was up to them, too, because they controlled everything.

They decided how you'd perceive everyone, and everything, around you. They made sure you'd never feel safe, wanted, approved, cared for, or normal.

The bullying was constant, and you had few, if any, opportunities to let down your guard and relax. Your abusers were relentless. They forced you to remain stressed and anxious every moment of every day. You had to continually look around corners, check your peripheral vision, and watch your back.

You had no contentment or peace. Your life was a waking nightmare.

Whatever challenges you may face now because of that childhood trauma, there is still good news. You have survived to this point. You've done that by virtue of your own hard work, faith, and strength. Credit yourself with accomplishing what you have.

Maybe some good things came out of the experience, too. You might have become determined and capable enough to fend off the next round of attackers based on what you learned. Also, you might have gained life skills that have benefitted others. Through your pain, you might have gained empathy. Perhaps you grew in compassion and kindness, and in your willingness to respond to the cries of people who were in trouble.

You might have found a creative outlet for your suffering. Maybe you developed a skill, talent, or craft that you otherwise would have ignored. Possibly, you've taken pleasure in it yourself and have been able to share it with others.

Potentially, you chose as your vocation, or embraced as your avocation, the opportunity to work with children, the elderly, the infirm, or others who have benefitted from your compassion. Perhaps you put much of your energy toward defending people who have few others who will support them.

Maybe you gained a healthy perspective about the people around you and the range of attributes that make us all valuable. Perhaps you became more appreciative than you otherwise would have been of the differences that make us all worthy human beings.

You might have become the type of person who defends others against abuse anywhere it occurs. Maybe you have a particular sensitivity toward advocating for, and protecting, human rights. Perhaps you champion animal rights and feel protective toward our environment and ecosystem. It's possible that, because of the bullying you experienced, you developed an impenetrable resistance to the lure of any politicians, leaders, or individuals who would marginalize, diminish, or torment subsets of the population for their own personal gain or sadistic pleasure.

Your capacity for goodness and caring, and the value you place on individuality and doing the right thing regardless of the cost, may be the rewards you have accrued for enduring childhood bullying. You didn't ask for the suffering, but maybe you — and the people around you — have reason to be grateful for it. Although you weren't able to choose the road you took, you may be satisfied about the destination you reached and how it helped you develop into the human being you are.

The Bully

You weren't always the target of your classmates. One person had to choose you as the target and had to set the abuse in motion.

This was the bully. He or she was the instigator.

When you remember the abuse you experienced, this is the person whose face you see first. This is the monster who appears in your nightmares.

Maybe the bully was once just a regular human being and appeared to be no different than any of your other classmates. But, somehow, the bully transformed him- or herself into your worst nightmare.

This happened through the bully's careful and thorough observation of you. The bully discovered your weaknesses and exploited them. This person was an expert at finding, and then pushing, your buttons.

The bully knew you pretty well. That is why the attacks were so effective and why they mattered so much. The intimacy between the bully and you lent a poignancy to the assaults they otherwise would have lacked.

The individual's competence grew through trial and error. Finally, the bully evolved into an unapologetic demon whose energies seemed devoted to singling you out for torment, ridicule, and destruction. Once the bully targeted you and ramped up his or her campaign, you never had a chance to make it stop. There was no escape.

The bully was probably a natural leader. Maybe this person was charismatic and popular. This was the president of the club that wouldn't accept you as a member.

Beyond the classroom, there might have been other clubs to join. But, while you were in school, this club was the only one that mattered.

It was the social club that would accept almost anyone as a member. All of its members were unified under the bully's leadership, and all of them had another thing in common: they excluded you.

That meant you are isolated and alone. Shunning meant the narrowing, if not the end, of your world.

Everyone aspired to be the bully's friend. Ironically, you probably wanted that at one time, too. You had the same social aspirations and needs as anyone else.

This bully might have been the life of the party. But you never scored an invitation. You could only watch from the sidelines.

Perhaps the bully was the hub around which all the excitement, life, and fun of the classroom revolved. This was probably someone you, too, admired at first and wouldn't have hurt for anything in the world.

Likely, the bully had a legion of followers. Hurting you enhanced the bully's social standing even further. Maybe the bully attacked you to impress others as much as for the sport of it.

The bully might have been the hero of a self-directed drama. The more the bully tortured you, the greater his or her marquee value was to everyone except you.

This might have been someone with whom you never had a disagreement. Perhaps you never even exchanged words with this person. The attacks might have begun so quickly and suddenly that you never had a chance to say a proper "hello," let alone to defend yourself.

The bully held all the power in your world. If the classroom was a country, this child was the ruler.

This may be the shadow figure who chases you in your nightmares.

You can probably see the bully's face and hear the bully's voice. You likely remember the bully's taunts and the tone of voice he or she used to hurl them. It is possible you can still hear the bully's mocking laughter.

If you close your eyes, you can probably still picture specific items of the bully's wardrobe: shirts, pants, jacket, or cap. You can probably visualize the way the bully walked. It is likely that you remember the bully's eyes, smirk, scowl, and gestures. You may even recall the bully's touch, and the smell of his or her breath.

Those may be images that you will always remember. Perhaps they horrified you so much, humiliated you so greatly, and frightened you so terribly that they will always be with you.

What was the point? Why did this person hurt you?

Perhaps it was simple. The bully might have been seeking some cheap and easy entertainment, and he or she might have selected you as the provider.

Maybe the bully tortured you because it didn't require much effort. Once the structure was put in place, and the original insults, catcalls, and threats were developed, the rest was easy. The bully didn't have to continually invent new material.

Maybe the bully was the class clown, and you were a prop. It's possible that the bully's abuse originally started out as a joke, a way to deal with frustration, or a break from the boredom of the classroom. Maybe the bully intended to just create a little bit of fun, tease you for a while, and then move on.

At some point, maybe the bully lost control. Perhaps, then, the abuse took on a life of its own.

Maybe hurting you filled a deeper need that the bully had. The bully might have had problems at home or academically from which you provided a distraction. Torturing a weaker kid probably made the bully feel stronger and more powerful.

It is possible that the bully was recreating punishment that he or she was receiving from a higher authority at home or elsewhere. Maybe the bully was acting out of frustration or helplessness. Maybe hurting you was therapeutic for the bully.

You might have been at the wrong place at the wrong time, and that is why the bully targeted you. Maybe something about you made the bully react. Perhaps you reminded the bully of someone or something else — someone the bully couldn't be, or something the bully couldn't have.

The bully didn't play fair. This person didn't even give you a chance. To the bully, you were roadkill. You had no rights, and you didn't matter.

In the classroom, the bully ruled absolutely. You were at the mercy of this individual. The bully knew it, and you knew it, too.

We're speaking about the bully as if it this were one individual, but maybe that wasn't the case. Possibly, a group of equally powerful people shared the role. One of them might have stood out as the ringleader. Or, maybe, there was a group of people who abused you, and none stands out as the main culprit. Perhaps the bullies were an undifferentiated mass of people who hurt you for no reason and whose memories continue to haunt you.

The Bully's Court

Your abuser didn't bully you in a vacuum. The instigator played to an audience, the most important members of which were his or her court.

These were the bully's most reliable allies. The members of the bully's court might have included the most beautiful, most athletically gifted, and the most socially adept students.

They might have enjoyed the admiration of those who ranked beneath them on the social hierarchy. Likely, they enjoyed tremendous popularity with the teachers, paraprofessionals, school administrators, coaches, and everyone else who worked in, or around, the school. Most likely, their own parents and the other children's parents thought they were simply wonderful. They might have flourished everywhere, succeeded at everything, and been the envy of nearly everybody.

Like all children, though, they might have had their vulnerabilities. While they were not as powerful as the bully, they might have aspired to be. They might have felt continual pressure to impress the bully and their other classmates.

Abusing you might have been their ticket to finding greater favor with the bully and the rest of the students. The more visible they were in their abuse of you, and the more enthusiastically they attacked you, the greater the amount of approval they might have received from their mentor and their classmates.

The bully's opinion probably mattered more to them than anything, since that was their leader. But they also needed the approval of the others in the class to thrive.

Their participation in tormenting you fed the bully's behavior and increased the bully's desire to hurt you. It also inspired and encouraged the bully. Their participation in the abuse might have been the fuel that kept the bully going.

It's likely that the bully's court acted as backups so that, if the bully was temporarily unavailable personally to hurt you, the tormenting could still proceed. These surrogates ensured that you never, for one moment, could lower your defenses and feel a modicum of safety.

These close associates of the bully might also have been leaders among the students. They might have enjoyed power-by-proxy, and perhaps hurting you was their ticket to ensuring they maintained their privileged position.

They used you as a stepping stone to get, and to keep, the popularity they craved. They didn't care about the fact that they were hurting your chances of living a normal life in the process.

Members of the court might have commanded positions of prestige and ranked only slightly below the bully. They might have basked in the bully's reflected glory.

Their actions might have been just as heinous as the bully's, but their motivation probably was different. Likely, it was far less personal, and more selfish and calculated. In fact, their tormenting might have been even crueler, because they might have been more conscious and deliberate in their actions. They might have known precisely what they were doing and why they were doing it. Their campaign against you might have been premeditated rather than spontaneous.

It was easy for members of the court to hurt you after the bully had ruptured your self-esteem and confidence. Finishing the job of shattering you probably was relatively easy, and it might have provided entertainment, novelty, and pleasure for everyone except you.

These popular children might have recruited other people to target you just for fun. The larger the club, the greater the rewards would have been for excluding you from it.

The members of the bully's court might have created their own techniques of abuse or, minimally, provided the bully with fresh material. They might have pointed out weaknesses in you that the bully hadn't noticed. Every time they found a new way to hurt you, their status potentially increased.

They might have encouraged the bully to continue a game that was no longer fun for him or her. Long after the person who initiated your abuse would have lost interest in hurting you, the members of the bully's court might have fueled the flames.

If the bully was the hero of the production, then the members of the bully's court were the costars. Their participation in your abuse served as validation that you deserved it.

It wasn't only the bully who thought so. The children who mattered most, socially, agreed. The jury was in, and they had found you guilty.

If it hadn't been for these children, the bully might have had a less enthusiastic audience. In the absence of the constant positive feedback the bully received from his or her closest associates for tormenting you, the abuse might have come to a natural and speedy conclusion.

It's reasonable for you to feel as horrified when you remember the behavior of these children as you do when you recall what the bully did to you. Perhaps, the memories of the bully's court are just as tough for you to deal with.

You probably remember the names and faces of the bully's court. It's likely that you can still see where they stood, where they sat, where they ate, and where they walked in relation to the bully and to you. You can probably still hear their voices, and you likely can hear the words and sounds they emitted to torment you.

In your mind's eye, you can probably see how they dressed. You can probably visualize the gratification on their faces, and in their stances, when they scored a direct hit against you.

These people, too, have their places in your nightmares. The way they once treated you probably also helped shape the way you have felt about yourself ever since.

The Followers

Beyond the bully and the bully's court were the other faces in the crowd. They weren't the most popular students in the classroom, nor were they among the ostracized.

Their special talent was their ability to blend into the crowd. They were the ordinary, unremarkable members of the class who went along with the bullying campaign and derived their own rewards from it.

Tormenting you was a way for them to show their team pride and prove their worthiness of club membership. Participation in the bullying may have provided them with some protection. If they were hurting you, they were probably exempt from bullying themselves. They might also have derived some pleasure from joining the abusers while incurring few risks.

They didn't initiate the terror. But, along with members of the bully's inner circle, they amplified it. They made sure you saw danger everywhere — in everyone around you, everyplace you went.

They did it because bullying you was a novelty and it amused them. It seemed like an innocuous way to pass the time. Fundamentally, following the leader was far easier and less threatening to them than taking a stand against the bullying would have been.

Granted, they weren't part of the bully's court. They probably didn't aspire to be. They were followers, not leaders.

But by approving of the actions and choices of the leader and the members of the bully's court, they became complicit. The play couldn't go on without an audience. The stars and costars would not continue to perform without applause.

Everyone occupied a place on the seesaw of bullying. The bully's strength was a foil for the target's weakness. That disparity enabled the bullying. The bully's inner circle enjoyed increased power through their close association with their leader. They, too, were more powerful than you were.

Followers, as individuals, lacked power. Alone, they probably weren't interested in hurting anybody. However, as members of the larger group, they possessed the required social standing and power to intimidate, terrorize, abuse, mock, and torture an outsider. Together, they were far more powerful than you.

Bullying may not have been wholly pleasant for all of the followers, all of the time. But participation in the club provided the benefits of power, protection, and inclusion, and the followers were willing to absorb the occasional pangs of conscience in exchange for those perks.

That worked for them, and it added exponentially to your pain. There were so many of them that it seemed they were everywhere. You couldn't escape them.

If only the bully, or the bully's court, tormented you, then you might have seen them as aberrations. But if everyone else thought you deserved abuse — if everybody said that you did — then everyone couldn't have been wrong. They couldn't all be scumbags. You must have been the one who was at fault.

You may still recall some, or all, of the people who made up the crowd of students. Perhaps you remember their individual contributions to your pain.

Or the names and faces of the followers may have blended into a blur of people who caused you harm and forced you to constantly look over your shoulder. They, even more than their leaders, probably convinced you that you were in imminent danger all of the time.

Their actions and abuse may still be an integral part of how you view the world and your place in it. They, as a whole, may still keep you off balance and frightened.

The Silent Bystanders

The onlookers were members of the crowd of students who didn't actively participate in the bullying. They did nothing to stop it, either. Their failure to take a stand when you needed for someone to step up fueled the campaign of bullying against you.

The silent bystanders watched as others targeted you. Perhaps they didn't enjoy it and wished the abusers would find something better to do. Bullying might have violated their moral code but, if they thought it was wrong or unpleasant, the silent bystanders didn't say a word, or raise a hand, to stop it.

In fact, they might have been powerless to stop the actions of the bullying. If they had intervened on your behalf, they might have been targeted by the bullies, too. Running interference for you might have seemed, to the silent bystanders, to be a pointless risk that was not worth taking.

The silent bystanders didn't owe you anything. It wasn't their responsibility to be martyrs. They were just kids.

At the time, there probably were no anti-bullying programs in place. They might not have been shown ways in which they could confront bullies or help those who were targeted. It is very likely that, even if they had wanted to do something, they would have had no idea of where to begin.

That said, the silent bystanders still might have provided you with support of some kind. They could have figured out something. Their silence meant that they were taking sides, even though it might not have felt that way to them.

By their silence, the bystanders helped the bullies convince you that no one in the world cared about you, and you didn't belong anywhere. Helping you, or at least offering you an occasional smile or a discreet "hello" when no one else was listening or watching, might have made all the difference to you. It would have proved to you that at least someone considered you to have worth as a human being.

It was particularly egregious that they allowed the abusers to hurt you, because they undoubtedly knew better. They did not treat you the way your tormentors did, and that probably indicates they understood that what the bullies were doing was wrong.

They understood the value of belonging to the club as evidenced by the fact that they refused to take the risk of doing anything that might get them bounced from it. Yet they sat by and watched while those club members ostracized an innocent person.

Their refusal to say a civil word to you was outrageous. Their failure to mitigate the effects of the bullying in any way, however slight, made them complicit.

And the fact that they were there, and they saw everything, made you feel horrified and embarrassed to be anywhere near them. You may still cringe when you think about the possibility of running into any of them in the present.

The Converts

Before the abuse against you gained traction, you might have begun to make some friends in the classroom. Also, you might have enjoyed positive relationships at school that predated the bullying by weeks, months, or years. These might have included long-term friendships. The former friends who joined the campaign of bullying against you were the converts.

These weren't strangers but, rather, people about whom you cared. You believed they reciprocated, and that they valued you and appreciated what you had given them: your trust and, generally, the best of yourself.

Inadvertently, you might have given these friends a direct line to your emotions and your vulnerabilities. While you were friends, you might have handed them the means to exploit you by sharing your secrets and memories with them. They knew your history. You had shared an intimacy.

Your tormentors sought to separate you from everything, and everybody, you cared about. They actively recruited your friends. It was important to win over to their side anyone who might have supported you so that you would be left with nobody.

The converts might not have gone over to the other side eagerly, but eventually, they succumbed to the pressure. They might have even wanted the rewards that would come with switching their allegiance from the class loser to the popular group.

When your former friends were converted by the people who abused you, they might have told you, or implied, that it was your fault. They might have made you feel as if you did something wrong, and the price you paid for it was their friendship.

You might have believed them. When your friends abandoned you, it was perfectly reasonable to think your actions provoked them. Something you did, or something you failed to do, must have caused the defection.

The loss of your friends might have made it difficult for you to trust anyone, especially yourself. It might have caused you to question your judgment of people. You might have felt unworthy of having friends and considered yourself to be incapable of maintaining mutually caring, trusting relationships.

When the converts joined those who bullied you, they might have waved the club's banner with more enthusiasm than any of your classmates. They had to work harder to cement their relationship with your tormentors and to prove that their loyalty was no longer to you.

Their former affection for you may have shifted to their devotion of those who were hurting you. Their cruelty might have been far tougher for you to bear than anyone else's, because what they were doing was far worse than simply abusing you. They were betraying you.

These converts knew better. They knew you didn't deserve to be bullied, yet they did it, anyway. Perhaps, they even gleefully tormented you or, at least, they probably made a show of enjoying themselves as they were causing you pain.

That spectacle probably destroyed you in a way that nothing else could. All you wanted was to feel as if you belonged and you were safe, and your former friends' conversion made you feel completely hopeless.

If your friends treated you this way, what could you expect of everyone else? If these converts had given you the one thing that was more precious than anything — their friendship — and then pulled it away again, then how could you ever get close to anyone again? And why would you even bother to try? The treachery of the converts, more than anything, probably convinced you that you were unworthy to be a part of any tribe.

They were the people whose abuse was most horrifying, because their opinion of you was based on an understanding of who you really were. The bully intimately understood the vulnerabilities about you that could most easily be exploited, but he or she didn't understand who you were. The converts did. And the converts couldn't have thought very much of you if they were willing to support the people who abused you.

The bully, the bully's court, and the followers worked together to spread their toxic opinions about you. The silent bystanders watched and did nothing. Your friends should have been motivated to do something.

They, at least, could have resisted the lure of joining the club. The value of your friendship should have outweighed the risks of incurring the tormentors' wrath. If the converts were so afraid of the others, they could have opted to join the silent bystanders if they lacked the ability to defend you.

These former friends had their reasons for converting, but they didn't tell you the truth about what they were. The fact that they didn't stick out their necks for you probably made you believe that you were the problem. If your friends didn't stand by you, then you most likely were not worthy of their support.

Perhaps the converts' betrayal caused you to shy away from friendships for years after the bullying ended. Maybe their behavior has left you fearing that, at any time, for any reason, your friends could desert you.

The Other Targets

Maybe you weren't the only child in the class who was targeted by bullies. There might have been others who were also scapegoated.

Because you had something in common — the abusers considered you to be roadkill — the other targets and you might have empathized with one another. It might have been beneficial to form a bond based on your mutual pain. You might have rescued one another or, at least, mitigated each other's pain.

That would have earned you at least one ally, if not a friend. The privilege of being someone's friend might have boosted your self-esteem and provided you with a positive focal point.

Maybe you generalized your fear of your classmates to every child in the room, even those who were also under attack. It is also possible that you couldn't differentiate between the powerful and the powerless because, from where you were sitting, they all looked the same.

It's even possible that the other targets in your class — who knew full well how debilitating bullying was — tormented you in a bid for a semblance of acceptance from the others. It's also possible that you bullied the other targets in your class for the same reason.

Perhaps, too, you viewed the other targets through the lens of the abusers. The children who were targeted by bullies might have seemed unappealing to you. Maybe you thought they were losers. They might have put up a wall of protection around themselves and exhibited anti-social behaviors. They might have lost interest in maintaining their personal hygiene or engaged in self-destructive behaviors, and their appearances might have discouraged you from approaching them. Perhaps you responded to the other targets' problems by avoiding them in the same way as others were shunning you.

Or maybe you did reach out to other scapegoats, and the relationship failed to materialize because you were out of practice. Maybe you could have tried harder.

86 · STACEY J. MILLER

Perhaps you could have forced the issue, if you had really wanted to. You might have been able to comfort the other targets and save them from some of their pain if you had stayed committed to pursuing that goal.

Maybe you gave up too quickly, and that might be something else for which you blame yourself. It might be that the positive relationship that didn't exist between the other targets and you is one of your greatest regrets.

The Teachers and Coaches

Here's what a competent teacher or coach might do if he or she spots bullying.

The teacher or coach might confront the bully, and tell the child that the behavior is unacceptable and will not be tolerated. By projecting authority, the adult in charge can let the child categorically know that bullying has no place at school and will never happen there again.

Skilled teachers and coaches can stop bullies in their tracks, and they will do it, instantly, at the first sign of trouble. They see it as part of their jobs. Dealing with children who are behaving inappropriately is part of what teachers and coaches get paid to do.

For some educators, maintaining a bullying-free zone seems to come easily. They appear to have been born with the skill, the way that some teachers and coaches possess stage presence, a voice that projects all the way to the end of the classroom — or a gymnasium, locker room, or field — and an ability to share the love of learning, striving, playing, and excelling.

Perhaps some of the great teachers and coaches had excellent role models when they were growing up. Their mentors might have helped them to excel at their jobs. Maybe the gifted educators learned as they went along. Perhaps becoming parents themselves turned them into determined, focused nurturers who would do anything to protect the young, vulnerable people for whom they were responsible.

But, when you needed a teacher or coach who would run interference with the bully on your behalf, you might have run into the other type. You might have found teachers and coaches who were clueless, incapable, and apathetic. The teachers and coaches you encountered might have had an uncanny ability to look the other way while you were being abused. Through their inaction, they might have given the bullies cover and even tacit approval.

Maybe they lacked the maturity or experience to handle the situation appropriately. It is possible that you caught the teachers or coaches at a bad time in their careers — when they had become bored or frustrated. Maybe they had become overwhelmed by the volume and scope of their responsibilities, and they just didn't have the energy for it anymore.

Likely, they felt that they worked too hard to handle additional tasks such as policing the children in their care. Probably, they felt they were underpaid, undervalued, and undertrained, and they might have been on the verge of burnout by the time you came along. Maybe, over time, the more aggressive children had become far too difficult for almost anyone to handle.

Some teachers or coaches might even have engaged in bullying themselves. It is even possible that it was the teachers or coaches, rather than the students, who initiated the bullying campaign against you. The teachers or coaches might have intended "only" to tease you or "bring you out of your shell" to entertain themselves or to elicit a particular response from you. Or perhaps they were performing for the pleasure of the other students who were captive audience members. Maybe they were even under the mistaken impression that they were doing you a favor by "toughening you up." From their point of view, maybe anything was better than allowing a child in their care to be a wuss or a sissy.

Some of these teachers and coaches might have experienced bullying in their own childhoods. They might have run away from their responsibilities, out of sheer terror, when they saw the bullies coming after you. Maybe they protected themselves by denying the reality of the abuse you were experiencing.

If that is the case, then what they did was selfish. They saved themselves the pain of watching young people suffering to protect themselves. In doing so, they left you alone and vulnerable. You were forced to deal with something the teachers and coaches opted out of.

These educators might have figured you would all live through the experience without any intervention, and they might have been right. But that doesn't justify what they did — and, more importantly, it doesn't excuse them for what they failed to do.

Teachers and coaches were in a position of authority and responsibility. They had no right to ignore the abuse, to participate in it, or to abandon the children in their care.

They signed up for the job. If it didn't pay enough, they had the option of changing careers. Staying in their jobs and allowing children to be hurt on their watch was not the right thing to do.

Teachers had autonomy in their classrooms, and coaches had control over their space, too. What they chose to do within their domain was strictly up to them. Looking the other way, abusing you, or deserting you was unacceptable. And, chances are, if they did any or all of those things, they did them with impunity.

Maybe your teachers or coaches felt miserable about the fact that they couldn't do the right thing and stop the bullying, and they might have held you responsible for their unhappiness. Maybe they resented the fact that you were causing them to feel as if they had failed.

They might have believed that there's always at least one person in every class or team who was targeted by bullies, and this time, you were the person who was chosen. That made it your responsibility to endure the ordeal just as countless other children had.

If you encountered teachers or coaches who were as intimidated by the bully as you, they might have yielded control of the class or team to that individual. This might have been the path of least resistance for them. You might have been under the jurisdiction of a teacher or coach who wanted to do the minimal amount of work for the maximum amount of pay, and who considered sticking his or neck out for a child who had been targeted by a bully to be beyond what the job required or the pay warranted.

They might even have convinced you that it was your fault. Maybe they prevailed upon you to consider why you were being targeted by bullies so that you could remedy the

90 · STACEY J. MILLER

problem. They might even have asked you what you did to provoke your abusers.

When you're a child, hearing something often means believing it. Perhaps you were convinced that you were being "bullied about" something. You might have bought into the concept that, somehow, you had done something wrong and elicited the abuse. If you felt you deserved the treatment you received, then you might have believed that self-hatred, guilt, and shame were appropriate responses.

Of course, you were never bullied about anything. No one is. Kids are bullied, period. Adding the word "about" blames the bully's target, and it implies that the person who is getting abused has some control over the situation. That is unreasonable, because bullying is not a valid form of feedback. Bullying is always illegitimate. If your teachers or coaches convinced you otherwise, then they did you a disservice. They might have done you lasting harm.

They also were either short-sighted or ignorant if they advised you to listen to the bullies and take direction from them.

What if the children declared that your skin was the wrong color, you were too physically developed (or underdeveloped), you had the wrong accent or speech patterns, or your sexual orientation or religion were inferior? Were you supposed to be able to change those things?

What if the children pointed to the fact that you used a wheelchair, stuttered, or were hearing impaired? Did they expect you to remedy those issues?

How about if they told you the world would be better off without you? Did they want you to commit suicide?

Adults never should have placed the responsibility into your lap for finding out why you were being targeted by bullies and then fixing the problem. That was as irresponsible as it was senseless. Teachers and coaches were supposed to be trustworthy. You expected them to advocate for you. Surely, with a teacher or coach around, a child wouldn't verbally abuse you or physically assault you.

However, they did. The fact that the teachers and coaches were unable, or unwilling, to intervene only emboldened the bully. Because of the teachers' and coaches' inaction, the bully's confidence grew. Once your attackers understood there was no consequence to hurting you, there was no stopping their behavior.

Teachers and coaches were professionals who had a job to do. They were supposed to help mold the children into productive members of society and prepare them to be contributing members of the workforce.

So what went wrong? These teachers and coaches might unsuccessfully have attempted heroics in similar situations, and maybe they were done trying.

Or maybe they had gotten away with doing nothing to help other targets in the past. The school year had ended, and the children had moved on. No catastrophe had occurred.

Perhaps they'd never had proper guidance about how to help students who were bullied, and they lacked the instincts to figure it out for themselves. They might have come to believe that it didn't really matter. Bullying happened, and it wasn't that big of a deal. Everything couldn't be their responsibility.

They were light years off the mark if they trivialized the campaign of bullying against you. In fact, you were in jeopardy precisely because there was no adult around to care. Any adult could have stopped the bullying.

Teachers and coaches were the people you had a right to count on. Perhaps the teachers and coaches in your life let you down when you most needed their help.

Maybe the teachers and coaches knew this. They might have felt terrible about failing you. Their unhappiness about what happened to you, and their role in it, might have stayed with them for years. It might never have left them.

Either that, or maybe there were too many children who were targeted by bullies who had come in, and out of, their lives. Perhaps these teachers and coaches never gave you another thought once you disappeared from their radar.

In any case, they probably remained on your mind. You can most likely remember their classroom numbers, where they stood or sat, how they arranged the students' desks, where they put their equipment, and even the outfits or uniforms they wore to work.

You may still see shades of these teachers and coaches in the faces of people in your current world who let you down when you really need their help. Every time an authority figure abandons you or anyone else, you may still feel remnants of the old pain.

The Administrators

Successful, well-adjusted students make school administrators look good. Students' achievements — academic, social, and athletic — reflect well on the people who manage the school.

Principals, vice principals, guidance counselors, and other school administrators have full plates. Depending on their positions, they may be responsible for managing teachers and other personnel; payroll; upkeep of buildings and grounds; community outreach; truancy; handling egregious problems at students' homes; counseling; and all manner of day-to-day housekeeping details.

They have more work to do than they have hours in the day to accomplish it. The last thing they want to deal with is a child who has been targeted by bullies.

School administrators aren't looking for more responsibility. Their doors are generally closed for a reason. Regardless of their job titles, they probably have no wish to micromanage students' day-to-day activities and woes. When a teacher, parent, or child pushes them to get involved in bullying, they may see that as an intrusion — a glitch that threatens to delay their routine and jeopardizes their sense of mastery.

A child who is bullied, in effect, may cause the trains to stop running on time. And administrators may deeply resent any child who is involved in that interference.

Administrators may have more interest in protecting abusers than their targets, anyway. It's a matter of numbers. The perpetrators vastly outnumber the children who are bullied. Combined, the aggressors have far more parents than the children who are targeted do. It is, therefore, more politically and economically beneficial to cater to the bullies than to the children they hurt.

Although, today, state laws require that schools have policies and rules in place to deal with bullying and cyber bullying, that was not always the case. Even if the school you attended had anti-bullying policies, the administrators might not have wanted to implement them. They might have believed things would work themselves out, and they had more important things to do. You were a pain in the neck, but chances were, you wouldn't become a legal liability.

They would only notice you when they had no choice. Of course, if you had anything to say about it, you would stay off their radar screen.

You wouldn't rat out the people who hurt you, because you knew the retaliation you might face. Also, what child would willingly go to the principal's office? You probably would never have visited any member of the school administration by choice.

If you were forced to go, you were probably upset, defensive, and uncooperative during the visit. The school administrators were likely even more hostile than you were, because they felt that you were confronting them or demanding something of them.

As a matter of fact, they might have been skilled at bullying themselves. They probably were well practiced at turning the situation around and blaming children for the suffering they were enduring instead of taking responsibility for the bullying culture at their school.

Your parents might have been involved. They might have advocated for you and pleaded for help from school administrators who were unprepared, unable, or unwilling to provide it.

The administrators' sole focus might have been on placating your parents with the least possible amount of effort. They might have said they would punish the abusers and prevent retaliation but never followed through. Perhaps they suggested you transfer to another school which would have been a case of the administrators' punishing you instead of the offenders.

Most likely, they did not suggest that your parents contact an attorney. Almost certainly, they did not offer to contact law enforcement to let them know you might be at risk.

At best, you were seen as a problem child. You weren't a part of the team. You had no school spirit. You had a bad attitude, and you were not an asset.

School administrators preferred to deal with children they deemed to be winners. You were not one of those golden students, and you offered nothing except the prospect of wasting the school system's time, energy, and resources.

They knew how to deal with children who broke the rules. If you required discipline, they could provide it. They were prepared to scold, punish, suspend, or expel you. They almost certainly had no clue about how to help you if you were suffering abuse, and they probably didn't lose any sleep over it.

Their priorities were simple. It was up to them to make, and to enforce, rules. They had to ensure the children formed straight lines, and that they moved briskly without running in the halls or damaging any school property. They had to pay bills on time.

The fact that you were being tortured, day after day, in the building over which they had full responsibility was an irritant and, frankly, so were you. They would have expelled you from their school system, if that had been possible. Perhaps they eventually found an excuse to do just that.

Your Family

Bullying wasn't something you could leave behind in the classroom. It was a family problem. You brought it home with you every day.

Your family members may, or may not, have been aware of any, or all, of the reasons why you seemed so different. But they surely knew that something significant was going on. Maybe they just wrote it off as a phase you were going through and figured you'd eventually work it out on your own. At home, as at school, you might have been anxious, depressed, unhappy, fearful, and angry. You might have constantly worried about what would happen to you when you had to go back to school.

You didn't feel safe at school. The time you spent at home only served as a reminder that your parents couldn't prevent people from hurting you the moment you walked beyond your door.

Even during weekends and school vacations, you might not have been able to let go of the pain and relax into activities that were unrelated to school. You might have abandoned your regular routines, given up your extracurricular activities, and abandoned your hobbies. Possibly, you spent much of your time in your bedroom with your door closed, glued to a monitor or a screen on an electronic device, and constantly blotted out the world with white noise or music.

You might have stayed awake, night after night, to postpone that terrible moment when you would have to face the start of another day. It's possible that you spent many of those hours, before you lost consciousness, wishing you would never wake up.

Even families that have a healthy dynamic do not always tell each other everything. If you declined to confide in your parents and other family members, your situation would have been typical.

You might have kept completely silent about why you had become reclusive and anxious. Maybe you considered your home to be the one place the bullies could not penetrate. Possibly, you didn't want to bring the bullies into your home. Talking about your situation would only conjure up, in your one refuge, all of the elements that were causing you so much pain. You did not want to invite the reality of what was happening at school to invade your only safe place.

Maybe you needed for your family to be your oasis more than you needed their understanding. Perhaps you viewed your family members as your only sanctuary, and you clung in desperation to their cluelessness, because it was all the normality that you had.

It's possible that you wanted to tell your parents all about your problems at school but didn't know how. Maybe you thought you shouldn't confide in your parents because you didn't want to cause them grief and stress.

You might have believed your parents would pity you if they knew you were being abused at school, and you couldn't deal with the potential drama. Possibly, they would call upon you to feel sorry for what they were going through, and you couldn't handle that on top of everything else.

You were ashamed to be targeted by abusers, and you might have been conditioned to talk about only positive things with your family. Maybe you thought you could handle your agony privately more effectively than you could cope with your parents' worry, grief, pity, hurt, disappointment, and shame.

Or maybe you never told your parents what was going on at school because you worried that they would interfere. They might talk to your teachers, coaches, or school administrators, and if your abusers discovered you had ratted them out, you would probably face retribution. You couldn't bear the thought of that. As bad as things were, you knew they could always get worse. At least you were still alive, for the time being. That could change, and you didn't want anything to cause things to escalate.

Maybe you did tell parts of your story to some of your family members, or maybe they ferreted out pieces of it by themselves. You might have asked them for help, hoping against hope that they would figure out some way to fix things for you.

It is possible they turned down your request. They might have believed bullying was no big deal. Maybe they thought that kids were just being kids.

If they followed the hackneyed script of other uninformed adults, they might have told you that, if you just ignored the bullies, your abusers would eventually get tired of tormenting you. They might have promoted the theory that the bullies were just jealous of you. Perhaps they told you that, someday, your abusers would grow up and see the error of their ways. Once they matured, you'd be friends. All you had to do was hang on until then.

Your family members weren't with you at school, and they didn't know how seriously you were suffering. They might have trivialized what you were experiencing. Maybe they suggested you join in after-school activities and reach out to potential new friends. It would have been impossible for them to comprehend, based on the limited information they had, how unhelpful those suggestions were.

They might have scolded you for taking the abuse so seriously. Perhaps they directed you to toughen up.

Your family members might have judged you as morose. Seeing your unhappiness, they might have blamed you for it. Maybe they accused you of having the wrong attitude.

If you had physical complaints or were developing self-destructive habits due to the trauma you suffered, they might have deemed you to be sickly or weak. They might have accused you of inappropriately seeking their attention.

Or maybe they didn't blame you at all. Maybe they were outraged at the authorities at your school who were allowing you to be hurt, and they were determined to do something about it.

Perhaps they did take a more aggressive approach based on what you told them. They might have called, emailed, or visited your school.

Maybe they said the wrong thing to school administrators, teachers, or coaches when they met with them. It's possible they delivered their messages angrily or inexpertly. You might have felt that your parents would have succeeded in getting you help if they had been more persistent, more politically aware, more articulate, more authoritative, more credible, or more demanding.

Or maybe they didn't meet with school administrators, teachers, or coaches at all. Maybe you asked them not to do so. Perhaps they responded to your fears about the consequences you might face if they tried to intervene.

You may resent them for giving in to your pleas. They were the adults, and you were a child, and they should have known better than to yield to your fears.

There's a possibility that you blame your family members for not intuitively knowing that something was wrong. You might believe it was their responsibility to, somehow, persuade you to confide in them. Maybe you're angry about the fact that your family members hadn't earned enough of your trust to enable you to lean on them when you needed them. Your parents were supposed to protect you. It might have infuriated you that they couldn't.

You also might have been angry at your siblings, cousins, or other family members who didn't understand what you were going through, or who scorned you for having problems at school, and whose lives were going on as they always had. Possibly, you envied your other family members the normality of their lives and felt excluded from the clan. Perhaps you were disappointed in your family members' unwillingness to stop everything to focus on your nightmare.

Maybe you still harbor grievances against your family members. They might have tried to help you and only made things worse. Or they might have looked to their friends and other parents for direction without receiving any beneficial information. They might have let you down badly, but unwillingly.

It's also possible that your family was part of the reason you initially were targeted by bullies at school. Maybe your family lived in the wrong place, or spoke or dressed in ways that marked them as distinctive. Possibly, someone in your family had a mental, physical, or developmental difference that made them — and by association, you — seem outside of the norm. If you had been born into a different family, maybe you wouldn't have been on the abusers' radar screen.

Or perhaps your family was at the core of the problem in another way. A family member — or an extended family member, or a friend of the family — might have been the first bully in your life. From that individual, you might have learned to respond in a maladaptive manner to people who hurt you. You might have been groomed to become a target for bullies outside of your home by the very people who were supposed to be the foundation of your security.

Perhaps there is a chasm between your family members and you that had at least some of its roots in your childhood bullying. You may be estranged from some, or all, of them. Or you might have worked through the separation and found your way back to them again.

Forgiveness is often possible, but it is not always the only — or the best — possibility. That gift is yours to bestow or to withhold. You are under no obligation to forgive anyone. You are the only one who can know when, and if, the time is right to let go of the anger, disappointment, and hurt.

Understanding is another matter. By telling your story, you may gain insights into your family's role in the bullying you experienced. Maybe you can see patterns that you missed and, eventually, gain a healthier perspective. It is possible that, by examining your family's role in the abuse you suffered, you can gain enough insight to begin to heal.

Your Salvation

When family couldn't provide you with the support you needed, your salvation might have come in the form of other people who stepped up to help.

This might have been a student who befriended you. This individual might not have taken orders from the bully or succumbed to the group's pressure to join in the abuse.

Maybe it was someone who offered you the opportunity to talk. Perhaps the topic of bullying, which otherwise consumed most of your waking thoughts, was not even on the table during your interactions. Maybe abuse was the elephant in the room, but you managed to avoid talking about it with your salvation.

That might have been this individual's most precious gift: he or she enabled you to think about, and discuss, other things. Maybe your salvation provided you with an opportunity to just be yourself and to feel like a human being for a few minutes on some days.

Your salvation might have helped you find some peace, contentment, and even humor in a stressful situation. The fact that this child was unafraid to be seen in your company, communing with you, might have been a small miracle given the choices your other peers made.

Maybe the child was only able to make a small gesture. Perhaps he or she offered you a smile once in a while or told you a joke. Whatever this child offered that was positive and friendly was important, because it let you know that there were still people in your world who wished you well. You weren't alone in the universe. Somebody knew about your situation and cared about you, anyway.

Perhaps you can recall a time when this child confronted a bully on your behalf. Your salvation might have been confident, frightened, or outraged ... but he or she stood up for you, regardless.

This child's decency and unselfishness might have touched you so deeply that your gratitude has stayed with you. It may have become a permanent part of the way you view the world.

He or she might have been the first hero in your life. Perhaps you think of this person every time you support someone who is marginalized or mistreated. Maybe you think of your salvation every time you support a political candidate or policymaker who believes that everyone is entitled to decent, fair treatment.

Or there might have been a teacher, coach, librarian, nurse, counselor, aide, custodian, or school bus driver who demonstrated concern and showed you kindness. These adults might not have been able to fix the bullying problem or change your life in any big way.

But knowing there was at least one adult who cared about what happened to you might have made a positive difference. This person might only have been doing his or her job. Perhaps this individual assigned class work, organized the group into teams, recommended books, took your temperature, drove you to and from school, cleaned the bathrooms, made lunches, or provided you with a safe space for a few minutes during the school day. That might have given you something to look forward to, and perhaps that bright spot got you through some days that, otherwise, would have been unendurable. Maybe that adult provided you with the small bubble of safety you needed to survive.

The adult might have singled you out for praise, offered you words of hope, and demonstrated to you that you were valuable to somebody. The decency of that one adult might have been your beacon when you needed faith that, someday, things could get better.

Any goodness you experienced from a child or an adult at school mattered even more because there was so little of it. It was not enough to offset the abuse that you experienced.

But the individuals who looked past the bullying and saw the person you wanted to be might have provided hope that, one day, you would live a life free of daily suffering. They might have been the best part of your world and, because of them, you might have learned how to be a better human being. All the gratitude you feel for them may feel as if it could never be enough.

The Setting

Every story takes place somewhere, and the childhood bullying you experienced probably took place mostly, or exclusively, in a school.

Maybe it's been a long time since you have seen it, but you remember how the school appeared from the outside. You may be able to see what the building, or buildings, were made of. You may be able to see the color of the facade, and you probably remember the locations and shapes of the windows and doors. You may recall the courtyard and anything that grew there: trees, bushes, or grass. Or maybe your school was surrounded by concrete.

Perhaps the building was surrounded by a gate or a fence. There might have been graffiti on the building or trash strewn around the grounds. Maybe you can recall some of the words, symbols, or objects that other children had left there as their calling cards.

You may recall the texture of the path that led to the school's entrance. Maybe your hands remember the texture of the door handle and how it felt to turn or push.

It's possible that you still pass the building and that it evokes painful memories every time. Perhaps you sometimes imagine how it would feel to open the door and walk inside.

You may recall the layout of the building. Maybe you can remember the locations of the administrative offices and other places that mattered: the entrance, the gym, the auditorium, the cafeteria, the library, the teachers' lounge, the bathroom, and the nurse's office. Go to each of those places, and any others you remember, in your mind's eye. If you concentrate, maybe you can see where you walked, sat, or stood. Perhaps you can remember the other people who were there, and whether they allowed you your personal space or crowded you. Maybe you sat, or stood, all alone.

Walk down the hallways again. Perhaps you can see the staircases and climb up, or down, the steps. Maybe there were cloakrooms or lockers, and perhaps you can see children's coats, sweatshirts, backpacks, lunch bags, and textbooks.

It's possible you remember where each of your classrooms were. Likely, you can recall one or more of those spaces more clearly than the others.

You may see the numbers on the doors. Perhaps you turned the door handles and walk inside. Maybe the doors were already open, and you just walked through the doorways.

If you focus, you may be able to see how the students' desks were arranged and where the teacher's desk was, too. Maybe the teacher rarely sat at the desk. Instead, the teacher might have stood in front of the class. Or maybe the teacher only made a brief appearance and then left the room. Perhaps the teacher was chronically absent.

You may see what you passed on your way to your desk, and maybe you remember precisely where you sat. In your mind's eye, walk over to your chair and sit down. Put your belongings where you usually would. Recall whether or not the desk opened, and where you would place your books, notebooks, pens, and pencils. Look around you, and see who sits in the seats around you.

Can you visualize the walls and floors? Do you remember their colors and textures? Were there blackboards, whiteboards, posters, or charts? Can you remember anything that might have been written or printed on them? Are you able to visualize the windows and any window treatments? What did you see when you looked through them?

You may be able to picture the clock on the wall and hear the sound it made as the second hand moved. Perhaps you can recall the sound of the bell that began, or ended, class. Was there a telephone on the wall? Or were telephones already mobile devices by the time your story takes place? Was there an intercom?

There might have been ambient sounds: the hum of the heater, air conditioner, or lights. It's possible you remember the smells of the classroom, too: disinfectant, mold, chalk, paper, body odor, shampoo, or soap. Maybe you can remember the scent of your fear.

The Events

Your trauma was real, and you may have spent years replaying the events. Maybe you've relived them in your nightmares. Perhaps certain anniversaries or current events have brought some of your memories to the surface and forced you to reexperience them.

It's also possible you've blocked out as many memories as you could. Maybe you believed it was unhealthy to dwell on the bad experiences you had, and you did your best to suppress them. Possibly, the process was unconscious, and you repressed the memories without even being aware of what you were doing.

Maybe you remember a few key events and the rest of what happened is only a blur. It is possible you have always wanted to forget all of what happened.

However, instead of pushing the memories aside, it may help you to recall the events and reclaim your story. You don't need to remember every detail of every moment you spent in school among the people who hurt you.

Instead, you may focus your attention on some of the events that you can remember comfortably. See whether these questions trigger memories for you. Possibly, some of the incidents you recall will be pleasant ones. Others will be anything but that.

Prepare yourself. Now would be a good time to center yourself through exercise, yoga, meditation, reaching out to someone who cares, or doing whatever gives you strength. Your story begins now.

Was there a time you can recall before the bullying began? Maybe you remember how you felt when the school year started. You might been eager to make friends, learn, and try new things. Maybe you were optimistic about what lay ahead.

Or, perhaps, you were anxious about starting a new academic year and, possibly, finding your way around a different school. Maybe you didn't know anyone, and you were worried about finding people with whom you could connect.

Do you remember the first few days of school? Did you meet children right away, and did you learn their names pretty quickly? What did you think of the strangers who surrounded you? How did you feel about the teachers, coaches, administrators, and any other adults you came across?

Who started the bullying? Can you remember when it began? Can you recall the first incident, how it made you feel, and how you responded?

Do you remember when other students joined in, and what they did?

How did you feel when you realized you had been targeted by bullies?

What were the first signs you saw or heard, and how did the abuse escalate?

Where did the bullying take place? Was it in the classroom, the halls, the cafeteria, the schoolyard, the library, the gym, the locker room, the bathroom, the school bus, or the path to and from school?

Bullies often use lies to slander the people they target. Did that happen to you? What was the misinformation that members of the group spread about you? What stories did they tell? What lies and exaggerations did they propagate? How did you find out that people were hearing those rumors, and how did it make you feel?

What was the verbal abuse like? Did the children mock you? Were there catcalls?

Did individual children say different things? Can you connect the phrases with any particular faces or names? Or was pretty much everyone hurling the same type of verbal abuse at you?

What were their words? Which taunts did they repeat the most?

Did the abuse get physical? Did members of the group throw things at you or grab your belongings? Were their gestures physically intimidating? Did they put their hands on you or make contact with any other parts of their bodies?

What did the students ask of you? How did they threaten you? What did they tell you that you could, or could not, do? What did you believe the result would be if you did not follow their directions?

Did you have a plan for dealing with the children? How did you try to handle the abusers? Were you at all successful in your efforts?

Recall a typical day. When did you have to be at school? Was there an area, outside or inside, where the children gathered before you were allowed to go to your classrooms? Can you see yourself waiting to go to your homeroom? Can you hear, see, or sense the people around you? What were they doing? Did their demeanor change when they noticed you?

Experience yourself walking to your classroom and sitting down. What happened when you got there? How long did it take before the abuse began?

What did you hear? How did you feel? What did you do?

Where was the adult in charge?

Did you say something? Were you thinking something? Did you cry or scream, or did you keep your feelings inside?

How did you get to and from school? Did you walk or take the bus? What happened during those trips?

What happened when you got home?

Did you participate in any activities outside of school? Did you get a respite during those periods, or were you targeted everywhere, at all times, by nearly everybody?

Was there a safe place, besides your home, where you could go? Did anyone there support you?

Did summer and other vacations provide a reprieve? How did you feel when it came time to transition from that situation and head back to school?

Can you recall the worst thing the children did to you? How did the incident start? Did it involve something they said to you? Was there a conversational exchange? Can you remember the words?

Did it go beyond that? Do you remember the specifics? How did you feel? How did you respond? What got you through it?

You might remember feeling as if you were in physical danger. Perhaps you were physically assaulted. Where did it happen? How? Who was the perpetrator? Was there more than one person involved? Did anyone witness the assault?

How did the period of bullying end for you? Did you see the experience through until the end and finish out the school year? Or did you somehow escape and leave in the middle? Was there an apocalyptic conclusion to the bullying, or did it just sort of fizzle out? What happened? Where did you go?

Whom did you hold responsible then? Has your perspective about that changed? If so, why? And how?

Perhaps your survival mechanism kicked in and, at some point, forced you to break the rules. You might have fought back when a child physically assaulted you. Maybe you sought out a forbidden area of the school for shelter. You might have arrived late to class, or exited early, in an effort to escape from children who threatened to hurt you at prescribed times. Do you remember fighting? How did that feel?

The teachers, coaches, and administrators who wouldn't provide consequences for those who bullied you might have willingly punished you. After all, disciplining a child who has been targeted by bullies takes far less effort than modifying the behavior of an abuser. Taking some sort of action, even if it was unfair and unreasonable, might have felt productive for teachers, coaches, and administrators who were ineffectual in almost every other way. Do you remember a time when a teacher, coach, or administrator confronted you?

You might have felt so helpless that you lashed out at others who were just as low — or, perhaps, even lower — on the social ladder than you were. Even though you were bullied yourself, you might have bullied others.

Just because you were suffering didn't necessarily mean that you were an angel. In fact, maybe your misery led you to behave in ways that you feel sorry about now. That in no way justifies the abuse that you suffered or undermines your right to tell your story.

Maybe you have always regretted some of the things you did and wanted to reach out to some of the people you might have hurt. It's rarely too late.

The events you recall may lack the drama of a Hollywood film. That doesn't mitigate the effect they had on the child you were.

During your childhood, school probably constituted most of your world. What happened there determined the quality of your life. The unhappiness you experienced, and the security and sense of belonging you lacked, set the stage for the trauma you may have experienced ever since.

Don't be tempted to trivialize your memories. Recognize the abuse you endured, and honor the ways in which you responded.

Allow yourself to remember any good memories that may unfold. Was there anything, or any place, you especially enjoyed? Was there anyone you loved? Were there animals you cherished? Were there aspects of nature that called to you? Were there passions that drove you?

What was involved? Did anyone share happy times with you? Allow yourself to feel gratitude for anyone who was there, everything that helped you feel whole and human, and whatever got you through.

CHAPTER EIGHT

TELLING YOUR STORY, PART 2

You know some, or all, of what happened during the time when bullying eclipsed everything else in your childhood. The memories are there: the characters, the setting, and the events.

This is your story. How you tell it, and whether you share it, is up to you. Do what feels best to you. Do not pressure yourself to do anything that pushes you beyond your comfort zone.

Telling your story can be therapeutic. It can be cathartic and liberating. Possibly, the act of creating your story can help you to release your pain.

But it can also retraumatize you, so proceed with caution. Go at your own pace. Be mindful of which rocks you lift. Prepare yourself for the unexpected and the overwhelming, and be ready to tap into your support system for help if your reaction to remembering the story of your childhood bullying is more than you can handle alone.

You may be self-conscious, especially at the beginning. That could be a positive sign, because it may mean that you're getting at the truth instead of hiding behind any defenses you may have built up over the years.

Go gently, and remember that you are the storyteller. This is your narrative. You are in charge.

You lived through childhood bullying. You know what happened. Maybe you hid some, or all, of the facts from others. You might even have lied about your school-related experiences when you were directly asked about them — even years later.

Perhaps you developed clever ways to gloss over things. You may have become the grand master of using euphemisms or just plain avoiding the topic.

Or you might have freely talked about it at the time, but at some point, stopped. Perhaps you told parts of your story, to some people, but you never told all of it to any individual. You may not have wanted anyone to be able to assemble all of the pieces and see the whole picture.

Maybe you took your storytelling as far as you could, and then you closed down again. You might have thought the stories of your childhood belonged in the past, and it would be unhelpful to revisit them or burden others with them.

Whatever your choices were then, you have a perspective now that you lacked before — even if "before" was only a week ago.

You can see things through a wider lens, and you can provide a more useful framework for your story than you were able to develop before.

Maybe, finally, it is just time. You are one of millions of people who experienced bullying at school, and you have the right to share your story.

You know that life goes on after bullying and that the power of childhood antagonists doesn't extend far beyond the classrooms of the past.

You may not see or hear about any of those classmates any longer. The distance you have traveled and the ways in which you have grown may provide you with a chance to tell the story with more objectivity than you previously could.

Also, you've almost certainly developed better communication skills than you had as a child. This will help you in your goal of creating your story — either entirely for yourself or for the purposes of sharing it.

There are several ways to create your story. You can take either an informal or a traditional approach. Within both, there are options you can choose.

Informal Approach

Just for Yourself

At the most informal level, you can create the story just for yourself.

You can recall the story silently, any time, and anywhere, you'd like. You can tell it all at once or in installments. Even telling your story one sentence at a time has value if that's what feels right to you.

It is not important to impress anyone. You don't have to tell the story in chronological order or to recount details that you're not able, or willing, to explore.

The story is yours to edit. You can highlight, or delete, any parts of it you wish. Literary devices, such as metaphor or allegory, may help.

Recall what you want, how you want. There is no audience you have to please. You don't have to recall every detail as if you've been hooked up to a truth detector or are the subject of a documentary.

You are not telling a story for its entertainment or shock value. You don't have to stun, horrify, amaze, or rivet anyone. Your story doesn't have to rival a movie or TV series.

In fact, what was show-stopping for you when you were a student may seem relatively banal to you now. You've followed the news. You've seen the effects of wars and unfathomable political choices. Most likely, by now, you have experienced the loss of loved ones, health scares, and other disasters.

Your childhood experiences may pale in comparison to global events such as 9/11, but that doesn't mitigate their importance or the impact they had on you. Your adult perspective doesn't trivialize the long-term consequences the trauma has had for you, and it doesn't lessen your need to tell the story. It doesn't mitigate the benefits you'll receive when you do.

The abuse of your childhood was all-consuming while it was happening, and you don't have to apologize for the fact that, with the passage of time, the edges may have softened.

Maybe the story sounds far less dramatic now than it felt then. That does not invalidate the potency of your story or its long-term effects on you. Nothing mitigates your right to tell it.

You don't need to fact check, either. Your memories don't have to agree with anyone else's. This is a story you're telling for your own benefit, and it is your truth. You can remember what happened your way, on your terms.

When you're ready, begin. You can write your story as a series of letters, poems, essays, journal entries, or articles.

Again, this is the most informal approach that you are now considering. You do not have to turn the telling of your story into a project that could take months or years. If you'd like, you can keep it simple and get instant gratification.

You can write a first-person or third-person account. Don't worry about the length, grammar, or style. No one will critique this. No one will judge you.

If writing isn't your strength, then you can digitally record your story. You can also use voice recognition software — which is available for Macs and PCs, and all mobile devices — to translate your spoken words into text.

You can tell your story as a narrative. If that doesn't appeal to you, maybe you can turn it into a work of fiction. Your story may take shape as a fairy tale or a fantasy. Maybe it could be science fiction or a dystopian tale.

In your story, animals may stand in for the people. The setting may be another planet or prehistoric Earth. You can turn the bully into an inanimate object. You can transform yourself into an action hero.

Employ any literary devices you choose. You can begin one way and then change your mind. Maybe you have more than one version of the story that is waiting to be crafted.

Or you could tell the story through the eyes of another character. After all, this isn't only your story. There are other points of view, too. As a child, you could only see things from your perspective. It may be helpful to tell the story through the eyes of another person who was there. Perhaps you can relay the story from the point of view of an imaginary omniscient narrator who saw everything. You may, instead, choose to tell the story from the bully's point of view. What was the bully's motivation? How did the bully feel? What were the bully's goals? How did hurting you help?

Perhaps you want to write a horror story featuring a cast of fictionalized characters. You would most likely have an array of models on which you can base the monsters. Maybe you can also create some heroes to include in your story. You control the plot and the ending, so you can safely explore your darkest memories ... and maybe even have a little bit of fun with them.

It's okay to be playful and to crack a smile once in awhile. You won't be undermining the seriousness of your topic.

Maybe you can pen a screenplay based on the events, actual or dramatized, that you experienced. For example, perhaps you'll want to take the opportunity to put our childhood self on trial. How might that play out? Who were your accusers? What offenses did you supposedly commit? What would be your defense? What would the jury decide?

Or maybe you want to try your hand at drafting a comedic screenplay. Many of the greatest comedians had angst-filled childhoods and found a way to turn their pain into relatable humor. Your work doesn't have to be filled with one-liners, and it doesn't have to be laugh-out-loud funny, but you can use irony and dry humor to relate your childhood experiences. Perhaps you can look to some of your favorite comedians for inspiration.

How to Begin

To begin the storytelling process, you may consider taking an actual, or virtual, trip back to your hometown. Perhaps you can gaze at your school from the outside and remember how you viewed it as a child. If you have the time and opportunity — and if you want to risk the possibility that you will run into familiar faces — you may want to request a tour of the building in advance of your visit.

It may be advantageous for you to walk, drive, or ride a bike around your old neighborhood. Perhaps you can trace the path from your childhood home to your school. When you feel the pavement beneath your shoes or your wheels, you can pay homage to the child you were and let the memories begin to unfurl.

Sharing Your Story Informally

If you decide to share your story informally, you can talk to a caring listener. That may be a mental health counselor, family member, or friend. Or it may be easier to talk to a stranger, as the fictional Forrest Gump does when he shares his life story with a random woman at a bus stop.

You don't necessarily need to sit on a public bench. Maybe it would make more sense for you to go to a favorite park, walking trail, restaurant, or food court of a mall — the type of place where you have a track record of running into strangers who are willing to have a conversation of longer duration than, "Nice day out, isn't it?" "Yep."

Some privacy may be helpful. But, obviously, you should never subject yourself to potential harm by being alone with a stranger. Find a place where you can talk quietly, and others can see you without overhearing your conversation.

You can begin by asking someone to provide you with a few minutes of listening time. Caution him or her that the topic is serious, and if you've never talked about it before, you should mention that, too. That will ensure that the person you've chosen is willing to be a sympathetic listener.

If you are sharing your story with someone you know, then you can ease into it more gradually by requesting that the person in whom you are confiding first read a book or see a movie that incorporates the theme of childhood bullying, such as *Carrie* by Stephen King or *Harriet the Spy* by Louise Fitzhugh. Choose a story with which you are familiar and that resonates with you, or share a news account of a bullied child with your confidante.

This will provide a common frame of reference. Once you're ready to have the conversation, you can highlight the parts of the novel, movie, or article to which you relate. You may point out the ways in which the story is similar to yours. Explain how, and why, you identify with the story and the people in it.

Discuss the differences between that story and your experience. Point to the place where your experience begins to diverge from the other. That's the beginning of your opportunity to share the way things were for you.

Perhaps talking to a person on a one-on-one basis is a more difficult place to begin than sharing your experiences online. Consider joining a Facebook group called Survivors of Bullying at School which is an inclusive community where members can feel safe in sharing their experiences. You may find similar groups on other social networks and social news sites such as Reddit and Medium.

Traditional Approach

If you want to capture your story in a more formal way so that you can share it with a wider audience, you may consider writing a memoir or a novel. The latter would allow you to fictionalize aspects of the story — such as names and places — to protect the innocent (or even the guilty whom you might feel a need to safeguard, either for personal or legal reasons).

You can write your narrative in chronological order, but you don't have to do it that way. It isn't necessary to wait until you figure out how to begin or until you're convinced that you'll do a masterful job writing your story.

Start anywhere. You can dive into the middle or the end, or you can plunge in months or years before the beginning. You can always edit your words later on.

Finding a Writing Community

Writing a memoir (or novel, screenplay, or any other genre) may seem daunting if you have not done it before. If you would appreciate some help, consider enrolling in a writing class. Udemy, Lynda (which is now part of the LinkedIn network), The Great Courses, and other online venues offer on-demand courses. You can participate on your own schedule and in private. Perhaps you could benefit from the ability to participate in only the parts of the courses you need, watch the course's modules more than once, or ask the instructor questions with anonymity.

If you prefer in-person learning opportunities, then search online for "adult education" and include your city or state. You will find organizations such as the Learning Annex that provide cost-effective writing courses. Your local library, high school, or community college may offer adult writing classes. You may also search online for "writing conferences" and "writing workshops."

Mingling with other writers, either online or in person, will provide you with the opportunity to intimately learn the craft of writing. You can give, and receive, critiques from an instructor and your peers. Other writers who want to tell their stories can provide you with support and may be willing to accept yours, too. At writing conferences and workshops, you will also have the opportunity to network and, potentially, to connect with a literary agent or traditional book publisher.

You'll find writing communities online, too. Check out writers' groups on Facebook, LinkedIn, Twitter, Reddit, and other social networks. That will give you an opportunity to network with writers who are working at every level of the craft. Among them, you are likely to find people who would be able to answer any questions you have or who can help you navigate your way through any literary challenges you encounter.

Alternatively, you can begin, and continue, your writing adventure on your own. All writing takes discipline and perseverance. However, it takes even more fortitude when you're tapping into horrible memories. It's important to have a process in place to keep your project moving along at a pace that feels comfortable as well as productive while accommodating your needs and prioritizing your comfort.

The Writing Process

Here are some ways to create a writing process that will be conducive to telling your story as productively as possible. Your comfort, too, is key.

Schedule time to write. Put it on your calendar. Establish a beginning and ending time, and commit to honoring that obligation.

Turn the place where you write into your own sanctuary. Place the objects you need around you. These might include books, photographs, candles, or an aroma diffuser. Remove clutter or anything that might distract you.

Free your writing time by taking care of your obligations first. Then you will be able to pursue your writing without guilt or fear of interruption.

Before you begin a writing session, clear your mind by walking or engaging in some other form of exercise, listening to music, or meditating. Do whatever you find most relaxing and energizing. Develop a ritual to ease yourself into a creative mood.

Turn off any electronic devices that might ring, sing, beep, or vibrate to get your attention. Eat, drink, and use the bathroom before you begin. Wear loose clothing. Come to your space ready to focus on the project at hand.

You may hear advice from books or instructors to rush through the first draft of your manuscript. Keep writing, they'll advise you. Do not hesitate or mull anything over. If you get stuck anywhere, just forge ahead and get it done. You can fix any errors or fill in any blanks later on.

That's true. Your writing does not have to be perfect, and you can edit anything you have written at any time.

Those who provide guidance often suggest that writers create an outline before they type, or dictate, a word. That provides the book's foundation and structure.

For many writers, that is sound reasoning. Having an outline to work from can simplify the writing process and keep the project on course. It can also be a workaround for writer's block which tends to affect most people at one time or another.

But, when you are writing the story of your childhood, you are confronting painful memories. You are reopening doors that may be rusted shut, and you are exposing yourself to unresolved trauma. Your priority is not to meet a deadline, race against the clock, or complete an assignment. Your mission is to take care of yourself while safely and comfortably conveying the story of what you endured.

Writing can be isolating under the best of circumstances. Penning your memories about the isolation of your childhood, and how it affected you then, can be a double whammy.

Take care of yourself. You don't have to announce to everyone, or anyone, that you are writing your story. But you can ask for understanding if you fall into a funk. You can request compassion when you feel plagued by sadness. And, if you need the help of a counselor, friend, or a loved one, you must allow yourself to reach out.

You may have become used to checking for emergency exits when you sit down in a theater or walk into a public building. Although you may never need to escape from a dangerous situation, it's important to know that you have a plan in place, just in case an emergency arises. When you're tuning into tragic childhood memories, it becomes similarly important to map out a fast and reliable route to safety before you need it.

Prepare a dependable way to calm yourself, or get yourself into your comfort zone, quickly. That may mean creating a playlist of favorite songs, having on hand the ingredients to make your favorite meal or snack, keeping your phone within easy reach so you can call or text a friend, or making plans to do something that will bring you joy.

Treat yourself with tenderness. Make time for what brings you pleasure and satisfaction. Manage your stress as you proceed so that it can't overwhelm you. Spend time in nature. Commune with pets. Watch silly movies or television shows. Express your love for the people who matter most to you. Help others, whenever and however you can.

Put your storytelling into perspective. While it is important, telling your story is only one part of your world. There is so much more.

Writing brings good days and bad days. It provides satisfactions and frustrations. Using your storytelling abilities for therapeutic reasons is wise. But remember to be kind to yourself, regardless of the outcome. You will learn over time. Show yourself the patience you would want others to give you. Manage the process with compassion. Encourage, but never push, yourself.

Proceed at your own pace. Tune into your instincts, and honor them. When you've had enough, take a break. You can pick up where you left off, or at a completely different point in the story, later on.

Honor your accomplishments. When you hit milestones, reward yourself. That may mean finishing a paragraph, remembering an incident, or typing a certain number of words — say, 500, 1,000, or 30,000.

You may not reach the end of your story. Distractions, challenges, or other important obligations may come up, and you may have to put your project aside for awhile. Perhaps you will need to gain some distance from your story to process what you've remembered and to deal with what you still have to convey. Or, perhaps, you will encounter a creative or technical problem that will bring you to a temporary, or even a permanent, stop.

It happens. Telling even part of your story is important. If you don't commit it all to writing, that's okay. You may come back to it when the time is right. Assure yourself that everything will happen just as it should. The only measure of success should come from you.

If, and when, you do reach the end of your story, be prepared to feel a range of emotions. You may feel euphoric. It is possible that removing a heavy weight from your shoulders will bring you instant relief.

Give yourself an opportunity to absorb the story you've told and to react to it. With a clearer picture of the tragedy you endured, you may find yourself grieving. That's okay. It's natural to feel sad for the child you were and for the pain that young person endured.

You may feel astonished that some people did such terrible things and others allowed it to happen. Perhaps you're feeling rage for the very first time.

Maybe you need to cry, scream, pound nails into wood, knead dough, lift weights, run around a track, or punch a pillow. Allow yourself to express your emotions.

Whatever you feel is okay as long as you are prepared to get help if you need it. Monitor yourself. Understand the boundaries of your danger zone, and know what to do before you feel overwhelmed or have reason to feel alarmed.

Your response to telling your story may be to celebrate the fact that you've freed yourself from those memories. It's okay to feel triumphant that you've accomplished what you've set out to do. You've recorded the truth, and you have denied those who controlled your past the ability to determine your future.

Now that you have dragged old, toxic secrets into the light where they can no longer hurt anybody, you have cleared a path for yourself to move forward.

Multiple Narratives

The story of the childhood bullying you endured may not have taken place all in one place or at one school. You may have multiple experiences to relate.

These events may have spanned multiple time periods. They may have involved different characters, settings, and events.

Once a bully targeted you, you may have been primed to serve as a scapegoat when any other individual or group of children required one. Therefore, childhood bullying may be a theme that ran through your past.

You can capture each of the stories at once, and you can let go of them all at the same time. Or you can focus on the story that weighs the most heavily on you.

Relieving yourself of part, rather than all, of the burden is a fine beginning or even conclusion. Shedding all of the excess baggage at the same time may be even more liberating. Do what feels best to you. Realize, too, that you can render your story using any art form you prefer. If painting, songwriting, drawing, sculpting, dancing, photography, making videos, creating animations, decorating, crafting, or scrapbooking are your preferred methods of self expression, then render your story in the way that best suits your skills, tastes, schedule, resources, and preferences. This is your story, so tell it in the ways that resonate most with you. You deserve to share the story of your hardest battles in the way, or ways, that feel the most rewarding.

Private or Public

Even if you have chosen a traditional approach to creating your story, that does not mean everyone must have access to it. You can choose to keep your story to yourself. Privacy is your right, and if you feel safest within it, then exercise that privilege.

On the other hand, you may find it is important to widely share what happened. You may decide that the best strategy for empowering yourself, and moving past the silence and shame, is to go public with your story.

Perhaps you are convinced that the story you once struggled so hard to hide now deserves to be heard. In return for telling it, you may hope for some relief and solace.

You may want people on the receiving end of your story to support and comfort you. Perhaps you believe that some of the people who read your story will relate to it and feel less alone — and will, perhaps, be able to survive their own childhood bullying and manage their personal trauma.

It is okay to want those things. However, if you decide to tell your story to others, the reactions you receive will not be within your control. You may find that your story is ignored or receives mixed reviews. It is possible that you will find people doubting, questioning, or even ridiculing your memories.

Those who were targeted by bullies were expected to endure it stoically and quietly, then they were supposed to forget all about it. Anyone who told others his or her bullying story was violating the code and threatening the system.

That attitude is beginning to fade. However, you may still come across people who feel that you should just get a handle on yourself and move on.

You may be sanctioned for telling your story. People may accuse you of wallowing in self-pity or dwelling in the past.

Our culture's insistence that you keep quiet about the abuse you experienced adds to your burden. Your silence is a prison, and your story is the key to setting yourself free.

You do not have to feed into the conspiracy of silence. Telling your story has always been your right, and unburdening yourself can be an important step toward finding closure and healing. However, there may be a price to pay.

As you seek people who commiserate with you and who will say exactly the right things, you may instead encounter people who wish to poke holes into your story. They may feel threatened by your truth, and that may motivate them to behave in unexpected and unpleasant ways.

They may question the veracity of your story. Possibly, they will accuse you of exaggerating. They may imply that things couldn't possibly have been as bad as you've made them out to be. They may question why you have to talk about such ugly things.

Some people may compare your story to others they have heard from those who have experienced childhood trauma and find that yours falls short. They may tell you that others have suffered far worse things than you have, and you don't hear those people complaining. Perhaps they will try to convince you that you should be ashamed of yourself for wanting to garner more than your fair share of attention and comfort.

As outrageous at those responses may seem, you would not be the first person who experienced them. In fact, you would be in good company.

When Oprah Winfrey selected *Night* — a memoir by Holocaust survivor Elie Wiesel — for inclusion in her book club, thousands of people around the world read (or reread) it. The life-affirming, courageous book received a mixed reception from those who found the book through Oprah's book club.

While most readers marveled at Wiesel's ability to survive such an unimaginable nightmare with his humanity intact, others questioned the reliability of his memory. They expressed doubt that Wiesel could accurately recount the specifics of incidents that had taken place decades before.

Historical revisionists accused him of outright lying. The autobiography that had demonstrated Wiesel's courage, strength, and resilience to most readers around the world was denigrated as a pack of lies by doubters and haters. To the latter group, human pain and suffering were apparently open to interpretation, and they weren't buying into Wiesel's story.

You do not have to answer to your critics any more than Wiesel had to answer to his. No debates, explanations, or apologies are necessary. You don't need to defend yourself to anyone. Those who feel entitled and even obligated to question your truth have their own problems, and solving them is not your responsibility. Their response does not in any way diminish the story you have shared. Telling your truth should be your only goal. External validation may come, but seeking it can lead to disappointment. The only person whose approval you need is your own. You are not responsible for teaching people to behave respectfully or compassionately.

Whatever people believe about the veracity of your memory, telling your story will still do some good. Sharing your story makes it just a little bit tougher for society to enforce its demand for silence. It ensures you are not complicit.

Your act of courage tells others who have experienced bullying at school that they can speak up, too. Telling your story may relieve your burden as it helps to change society's vision of the appropriate response to bullying.

Publishing Your Story

If publishing the story is your goal, you can solicit help from members of a writers' group or a developmental editor.

Self-publishing is probably the quickest path to publishing your story. If that is your mission, then Amazon's CreateSpace (which is a print-on-demand service) and KDP (which is Amazon's digital publishing arm) make it relatively easy and inexpensive to self-publish trade paperbacks and ebooks. They also provide distribution for books and ebooks which means, once you approve your book and ebook (you're able to review the materials first), your book or ebook can be made available via Amazon and most other online sales channels you choose.

CreateSpace also give you the option of making your book available only to you. In other words, you can go through the process of setting up your account, and uploading your book cover and the interior book pages file.

Once CreateSpace processes your files, they make your book available for your review. Your account then awaits an action from you so that you can see and, potentially, approve your book. Ordinarily, you would then select the sales channels you prefer and give CreateSpace permission to sell your book through its website and via Amazon. Then you allow CreateSpace to retain the right to distribute your book.

However, it's possible to keep your book in your account without providing CreateSpace with the ability to sell it to anyone except you. You can publish your book, and order printed copies for yourself and others while the book is published, and then you can change the book's status to inactive.

It's relatively easy, and free, to set up CreateSpace and KDP accounts. You can begin the process in advance of having a finished manuscript as a way of assuring yourself that your project is important and you are committed to completing it.

During the process of setting up your book and ebook on CreateSpace and KDP, you will be asked to provide author information. You certainly can use your own name.

CreateSpace and KDP will need your actual name and bank account information (for tax purposes, anyway). But once you've set up your CreateSpace and KDP accounts, and you're beginning the process of uploading your book and ebook, you can choose to use a pseudonym instead of your actual name. That will provide you with anonymity in the event that you want to tell your story but decide you would rather not go public with it.

If you choose to use your real name and make your self-published book available to the public, be sure that you've first cleared your use of any actual names and places with legal counsel. Ensure that you are not vulnerable to a lawsuit from people who feel you may have compromised their reputation and cost them money. It would be tragic for the perpetrators and enablers of the childhood bullying you experienced to be able to cause you additional grief by filing a lawsuit against you, so make sure to cover yourself legally before you publish anything — even though every word of it may be the truth, as you see it.

Amazon and its subsidiaries aren't the only options for distributing your book, either. You may also consider working with IngramSpark as an alternative to Amazon. Interestingly, one of IngramSpark's distribution partners happens to be Amazon. Since IngramSpark charges a fee, you may wonder why you should pay IngramSpark to distribute your book when Amazon's subsidiaries will do it for free. However, setting up an IngramSpark account along with a CreateSpace or KDP account allows you to place your metaphorical eggs in more than one basket and may expand your book's visibility in the marketplace.

People with little or no experience in book publishing self-publish their work every day. You can do it, too, if you have the willingness and patience to learn how — or the resources to engage someone else to take care of all the details, besides writing, for you.

Many independently published authors have written books about how to join their ranks. Check your local library for the most recently published titles, since the technology and business arrangements seem to change on a daily basis. You'll also find books that tell you how to outline your story, write more quickly, and maximize your book's profitability potential. Be aware, though, that few self-published authors earn money from their writing. The primary value you'll gain from self-publishing almost certainly will be the opportunity for healing, catharsis, and closure rather than extra income.

Most self-published authors spend money to publish their books and receive no financial return on their investment. Few people are able to handle all aspects of self publishing on their own, although some are able to navigate their way through most of the book production process themselves at little, or no, cost.

For example, CreateSpace and KDP offer free templates for creating interior pages and covers. Book Design Templates sells low-cost book covers and do-it-yourself interior page layout templates. They also provide a range of book production services in case you do not want to slog through the technical aspects of self-publishing a book. Other companies and individuals are available for hire, too, at all price points. You can find them by searching online for "book designers" and "book cover designers."

Even for experienced writers, it is nearly impossible to create an error-free manuscript. So if you want to create a book free of organizational glitches, grammatical or word usage mistakes, word drops, sentence fragments, and typographical errors, seek out a copyeditor and proofreader. Conduct an online search for "book editing services," or use a freelancers' site such as Fivver.

Alternatively, you can engage a company that will do all of the book production and editorial work for you. They can also print and distribute your book. You may have heard of iUniverse, Xlibris, and AuthorHouse, but there are also lesser known options such as Lulu and Outskirts Press. An online search for "compare self publishers" will steer you toward resources for learning the pros and cons of each of these, and many more, fee-based book publishing companies.

The most expensive way to self-publish a book is also a truly hands-free approach: hire a book packager (also called a book producer). Book packaging companies bring together all of the services that are required to produce, print, and sell your book. They can even provide a ghostwriter or collaborator, if you need one. That might be the best option if your financial resources are greater than your interest in learning about the business of book publishing. A book coach can take the guesswork out of finding the right book packager.

Many authors also sell their stories as audiobooks (in addition to, or instead of, making them available as printed books or ebooks). Do a search on "Audiobook Creation Exchange (ACX)" for details about how to make that happen. You'll find that ACX allows authors to record their books themselves, or they match authors up with voiceover artists who provide the recording for a fee. Several business arrangements are available for your consideration.

CHAPTER NINE

OPTIMIZE YOUR ONLINE PRESENCE

Before the days when almost all biographical information was digitized and everyone had easy access to it, people from the past would most likely stay in the past.

Where else could they go, and how would they get there? They couldn't time travel, obviously. They couldn't twitch their noses or blink in a magical way to pay a visit to anyone, anywhere in the world, at any time. However, that essentially is no longer the case.

Now, people who haven't seen each other in years, and even decades, can take a virtual trip back to the past find each other online in the present.

That provides opportunities for all of us. We may run into old friends unexpectedly, and it can be a nice surprise when a distant relative or long-lost associate suddenly reemerges.

But the door swings both ways. Knowing that people who hurt you in the past might be able to find you again can compromise your peace of mind. You may find it a deeply unsettling proposition and wish you could avoid forever that moment when a former abuser ambushes you.

Before the digital age, keeping a low profile and staying nearly invisible seemed easy. By default, once you put people behind you, they'd stay there. You could sever relations with people you no longer wanted to know, and they would no longer have access to you, if that's the way you wanted it. You could change your phone number and keep your new one unlisted. It was possible to move and leave no forwarding address. If you were motivated enough, you could ask family members and the people in your inner circle to keep your location and phone number private.

In those days, tracking someone down would take serious work and skill. Depending on your skills for staying undercover, it might have been necessary for a person who wanted to find you to hire a private detective. That might have been prohibitively expensive and time-consuming — and, frankly, extraordinarily creepy — so you could probably assume that most people wouldn't go to such lengths to find you.

The internet has changed that. Even if you have not joined any social networks, created a blog or a website, or published anything you're written or recorded, a search engine probably could turn up your name, whereabouts, and contact information.

Articles that can shed light on what you're doing and suggest ways to find you are permanently archived. Anyone can search databases by keywords, and if the library can't provide a free copy of the article, the publisher probably will be able to scare up a copy either for free or at a minimal cost — all while the person who wants to find you is sitting at home (or anywhere he or she can use a laptop or mobile device).

Nearly all newspapers have established an online component with a searchable archive. Free and low-cost online databases abound that contain people's public records. What it means, for practical purposes, is that most of us can track down information about each other without much outlay of effort or money.

Many businesses maintain online directories of employees, and schools may maintain digital lists of their graduates. If you own a company — or you actively sell, market, or promote any product, service, destination, client, or point of view — you most likely maintain at least one website, blog, or social profile of your own. In fact, if you care about much of anything — current events, politics, your community, etc. — you probably participate in at least one online community.

Anyone can find you. It probably wouldn't cost people from your past more than a few minutes of their time to learn where you are, how you spend your time, with whom you associate, whether you have a family, where you work, and the best way to get in touch with you. It's so easy to find most people online that even those with only a passing interest in somebody may be tempted to look them up.

You can no longer hide. Names and faces you had hoped to never come across again may pop up in your inbox anytime.

People from your past may surface when you least expect it and when you feel least prepared to deal with it. Everyone is out there. Trying to stay invisible to even casual internet sleuths would sap your energy, and probably leave you stressed and frustrated. More importantly, putting your effort into shielding yourself from discovery online would deprive you of opportunities.

140 · STACEY J. MILLER

Trying to eliminate all online traces of yourself in the hope of hiding from people probably wouldn't work, anyway. Anyone who wants to find you almost certainly will be able to do so. It may be just a matter of time before at least one of the people from your past connects with you.

Since it's going to happen, anyway, you may as well take the attitude of, "Bring it on!" Instead of living in fear that abusers from your childhood can catch you off guard, be ready for them. You may even look forward to it, since the people from your past can bring with them the possibility of healing and closure.

Why They May Seek You

Maybe the antagonists of your childhood will want to find you because they'd like to hurt you again. That is something you probably have already considered. It is possible, but it is unlikely that the abusers you once knew are still intent upon tormenting you.

And, even if they do want to hurt you, that doesn't mean they *can*. Now that you are an adult, you have coping skills that weren't available to you when you were a child.

Also, when you were a child, you could be forced by circumstances to endure the bully's abuse. As an adult, you no longer have to sit in a room or share space with someone who wants to torture you. Nobody can command you to interact with anyone against your will.

So even if bullies from your past do want to find you in order to hurt you, their actual power to do so is vastly diminished. They probably are smart enough to figure that out for themselves.

Therefore, it is far more likely that, if abusers from your past want to find you, their reasons will be benevolent. Maybe they will simply be curious about you. They may wonder who you have become, and what you have done with your life.

People put their own spin on things. Maybe some former classmates remember you only vaguely and don't recall hurting you. If they were among the silent bystanders, maybe they hold themselves blameless for what happened.

Maybe they remember only bits and pieces of the past. They may have only shadow memories of you and what you endured, but are frankly curious to see how things turned out. It is possible they remember just enough to want to make sure that you are okay.

Or maybe they remember everything and feel the need to reach out to you to make amends. They may be working through a 12-steps program that encourages it.

Possibly, they are haunted by their memories of their own behavior and they, too, want to heal. Maybe they want you to provide them with the opportunity.

It's possible they want to convey a message to you. If that's the case, then maybe — not necessarily, but maybe — it would be in your best interest to hear what they have to say.

It's possible that, by listening to their feelings and needs, you can find some answers you would find helpful. Hearing the story of your shared childhood from their point of view can widen your perspective and provide missing pieces to some aspect of the abuse that has always puzzled you. Ultimately, making the most sense possible of what happened can help you let go of it.

It's also possible that, by providing people from your childhood with the opportunity to create a happier ending to the story, you can coauthor an alternate ending that you all will have an easier time living with.

Since people with even a modicum of resourcefulness and technical prowess can probably find you online, anyway, you may want to take proactive measures to determine what they will see when they do locate you online. Once, your tormentors might have been able to define how people saw you. Perhaps they even were able to determine how you saw yourself, but that no longer has to be true.

Nobody except you gets to decide who you are. You are the only person who has a right to define yourself. With that understanding, you can create and manage your online presence so that people who search for you will find exactly what you want them to see.

Expanding Your Online Footprint

For professional or social reasons, you may already have created an online presence and optimized it for search engines. If you have been successful at doing so, then you have helped make it possible for people to find you so they can consider buying a product or service you sell, hiring you, getting to know you, or supporting your project or mission.

You might have put a great deal of time and thought into creating an online platform for yourself. Perhaps you even have hired designers, copywriters, and search engine optimization specialists to help you create and maintain the image you wanted.

It is likely — perhaps even inevitable — that the abusers from your past will eventually research you online, but there is no need to dread it. You do not have to be a sitting duck and fear the intrusion.

Technology can be empowering. Whereas once you were helpless to determine how other people perceived you, it is now up to you to create the image they will perceive. The internet is at your disposal. You can embrace the opportunity to turn your online presence into a celebration of the best of who you are.

Maximize your online presence, and increase the possibility that people will find you. Ensure that, when people find your online presence, it sends a powerful message. Decide what people from your past should see, hear, and feel when they run across your online persona.

Celebrities would call it reputation management. Business leaders would refer to it as building brand. It all comes down to one thing: controlling what people discover about you when they find you online.

You can expand your online footprint so that it speaks to the abusers and others who were part of your childhood experiences, along with everyone else who wants to know who you are. Your online profile should convey exactly what you want to reveal about yourself.

Create an online hub, if you don't have one already. This may be your website, blog, or Facebook page.

You can use GoDaddy, Wix, Squarespace, Weebly, or similar low-cost services to design and host a website. Blogger or WordPress can provide creation and hosting services for your blog. All of these resources are relatively painless to set up and use, even for beginners.

They were intended to be user friendly. If the logic of one eludes you, try a competing service. You may find another set of instructions and a different interface easier to grasp.

You probably already have a Facebook presence. Updating your profile may be the easiest way of all to have, and manage, your online base.

Once you have an online hub that projects the messages you want to send, establish spokes of content that lead outward from it. The more spokes (that is, the more content) you create, the larger your online footprint will be. The larger your online footprint, the more easily people will find the persona you have developed.

Maybe you want the people from your past to realize that you not only survived the bullying of your childhood, but you are thriving. Your online persona can show them that you are embracing life and living it to the fullest.

Or perhaps it's important to demonstrate how you are contributing to society, personally or professionally. You may want to show off your children, travels, artwork, or hobbies. Perhaps you want to emphasize your beauty, wealth, academic achievements, or social accomplishments.

Maybe there are other things that you want to communicate or to prove. Whatever they are, you may want to convey them through text, images, audio, or video. Use whatever combination you prefer. The more formats you choose in which to deliver your messages, the larger your online footprint will be. That increases the chances that people will be able to find the content you have planted.

Put some time into optimizing your social presence for search engines, much as you would if you were trying to help potential employers, clients, or people with common interests find you online. Learn which social networks rank most highly in Google and other search engines, and focus your attention on leveraging them. Use keyword research tools to analyze which words you should prioritize in your tags. Expand beyond Facebook, in other words. Explore what else is out there.

If you haven't updated your other social profiles recently, you may be missing opportunities to take control of what people see when they find you. Go for it ... instead of trying to hide, do your best to let others find you.

Your updated or new social network profiles should include your maiden name, even if that's no longer part of your legal name. To ensure your personal safety, do not include your current street address or phone number.

You may want to create and publish an email address specifically for social media instead of using your regular email address. Gmail, Yahoo, and other providers offer free email addresses. Remember to check your new email address regularly so that you don't miss any emails and because dormant free email addresses have a tendency to be automatically deactivated if you ignore them for a long enough period of time.

Project confidence in the online profiles you create, and be honest. Be comfortable with everything you've represented about yourself, and take responsibility for its accuracy.

You can pick and choose the most flattering photos, videos, podcasts, accomplishments, goals, and so forth. Be selective. You don't have to blurt out every single detail about yourself, and let the world know about every meal you've eaten or every single photograph you've taken. At the same time, telling the truth about who you are will enable you to rest easy with your online profile.

Set your profiles as public and keep privacy settings as low as you can without jeopardizing your feeling of safety. You

146 · STACEY J. MILLER

can upload pictures from your childhood so that people from your past will be able to make a positive identification. Make it clear which schools you attended, and specify the city or town where you lived. Ensure that, to anyone searching online who may not have seen you in many years or even decades, your social profile unambiguously belongs to you.

To make it even more likely that people from your childhood can find you, join online alumni groups for schools you attended and for schools from which you know (or assume) your antagonists graduated. Some social networks, including Facebook, LinkedIn, and Classmates, may allow you to join groups of classmates as a friend, even if you were neither a member of the graduating class nor an actual friend.

Increase the odds that people can find you easily by broadening your online presence even further. Publish articles and personal essays on such venues as Medium and LinkedIn. Tweet the links to your published articles. That will increase the odds that search engines will index them. Leave trails of digital breadcrumbs that lead from your articles and essays back to your online hub.

You can create an Instagram account or a Youtube channel. Or you might create podcasts that you can host on SoundCloud or BlogTalkRadio. The more media you create, the larger your online footprint will be. But build only the channels you can maintain and to which you will enjoy adding content on a regular basis.

Go narrow rather than wide. It's better to stay active on a couple of networks than to contribute less regularly to many. Creating and abandoning a channel may only confuse people who are trying to find you.

Whichever spokes you create for your online hub, you should schedule time to design posts or content for them at least weekly. Make it a habit. You can maintain your social media presence in such a way that you'll be proud of what people will find when they search for you.

When They Find You

These search engine optimization strategies can be highly effective. All of your efforts may pay off. Once you've optimized your online presence, it may bring some of the people of your past to you.

Be ready for that. Know, in advance, what you will do if a message appears in your inbox.

Imagine it has already occurred: someone from the past has reached out to you. What happens next? That's up to you.

Just because you have put your profile online and someone from your childhood has found it doesn't guarantee that it's a good idea for you to respond. You have to determine your next steps on a case-by-case basis.

Your online world is your kingdom. Anyone can knock on the door, but you possess the only key. It's solely up to you who gains admittance.

Do what's best for you. It's your moat and your drawbridge.

You can call upon your inner child for guidance in making the admit/exclude decision. The child inside of you is the part of you that was hurt. Therefore, that aspect of your being has the right to express an opinion.

The child may be frightened and urge you to be cautious. Or the child may be eager to run ahead of you and explore the possibilities.

Honor the child's feelings. Hear that child's needs, fears, and hopes. The child inside of you probably has more direct access to your instincts than you do. That can be important. Consider the path that the child illuminates for you, but decide whether or not to traverse it based on your adult wisdom.

Ultimately, you have the responsibility of being the adult who thinks through the potential outcomes of revisiting the people who populated the awful period of your childhood. Ultimately, you have to make the decisions that feel right to you.

This is a good time to call in help from other adults. Take under serious advisement what members of your support network — including a mental health professional, if you're working with one — have to say. They care about your well being and will want what's best for you. Their insights are valuable because they know you well.

Perhaps they have heard the story of your childhood abuse. If so, they may understand how it affected you at the time, and how it still does.

As you discuss your options, realize that this isn't an all-or-nothing proposition. You do not feel equally threatened by every person from your past, and the intensity of your feelings toward them may vary. They are individuals, and you do not have to respond in the same way to each of them.

The bully, the bully's court, the followers, the silent bystanders, the converts, the other targets, the teachers and coaches, the administrators, and even members of your family and your salvation are not automatically entitled to enter your space and interfere with your peace. Each character from your story played a unique role. Consider each of them on an individual basis.

Sometimes, people change. Their life circumstances may be better now than they were then. Troubled children can become healthy adults. Those who wronged others may feel remorse. You could be doing a good deed if you were to listen to what they had to say. You are under no obligation to empathize with them, but hearing what they have to relay may benefit you. An apology from them may help you find peace. Perhaps offering you that apology will put them on a path toward finding relief from their guilt, too.

However, under no circumstances do you have to subject yourself to abuse from the people of your past, or anyone, ever again. Just because people can find you online does not mean they have the right to hurt you. It was wrong then, and that will never change. The civility that may have become your habit in adulthood is not something you have to extend to everybody.

Use the life experience you've gained since your childhood and the wisdom of members of your support network to decide whether, when, and how you will respond to anyone who reaches out to you — before it happens. Consider again the cast of characters: the bully, the bully's court, the followers, the silent bystanders, the converts, the other targets, the teachers and coaches, the administrators, members of your family, and your salvation. Contemplate the possibility that any of those people might contact you, one at a time. Rehearse what your response might be.

You can change your mind. No decision you make now is immutable. The key is to never let them take you by surprise.

Commit yourself to staying within your comfort zone every step of the way.

No one appreciates a sneak attack. You would not want a monster who has been hiding under the bed for years to jump out and surprise you. The issue may lie in the ambush rather than in the reconnection. If you're the person who is holding the remote control, it can be far more enjoyable to watch the show.

Prepare yourself for the possibility of crossing paths with the people who populated your story. The best way to do this is to find your former foes first. Watch and consider them — from a safe distance.

CHAPTER TEN

FINDING YOUR FOES ONLINE

The internet can be a healing machine. It has made the world so much smaller than it used to be.

The digitization of nearly everything has ensured that you can probably find some of the people from the past, if you'd like.

Before the advent of the online universe, that would have taken a great deal of work. It might have been prohibitively expensive.

Sure, you might have remembered some, or most, of the people from your past. Perhaps you would even obsess about the roles they played in your development. But unless you picked up a telephone book, and dialed or pushed numbers (or wrote and then snail-mailed a letter), you most likely would never have run into those individuals again. You would never have known anything about their present lives.

They might have haunted you, and your memories of them might have affected your present day choices and behaviors, but they would have to do it from a distance. After enough time had passed, the likelihood of finding out where these people lived, or what had become of them, was probably reduced to almost zero for all but the most tenacious seekers.

That might have been good, in some ways. The past stayed in the past, and maybe that was where much of your history belonged.

However, the digital world has provided you with the ability to connect with most of the individuals who were part of your life. Losing touch with the people who populated your past is no longer as simple as putting time and distance between you.

If you have maximized your online presence, or anybody in your family can be found online, then you are just a few clicks away from nearly everybody you've ever known. Social networks are eager to suggest connections for you based on your school, work, and community affiliations.

That can all become an advantage for you. The ability to find people from your childhood can become part of your healing process.

You will want to map out a strategy for facing foes on your terms. Since the web has brought about myriad opportunities to find people, you can use that as a chance to face your past and break the hold that it may have on you.

The internet has unlimited potential to help you work through old hurts and find a way to move forward with a clear slate. It can serve as a healing machine by allowing you to locate your childhood tormentors and face them online.

Shrinking the Monsters

Bullies from your childhood can be even more threatening when you remember them as an adult than they were when you experienced their abuse as a child. With the passage of time, they may have taken on superhuman qualities, in your mind. Your fear of them may have grown exponentially. In your mind, they may have become demons with unstoppable power.

You can reduce the monsters to their appropriate size and place in the universe by seeing where they are now. Their pictures, professional profiles, and biographical information are likely easily attainable.

It is possible that you can find their social network profiles online. More than three-quarters of the U.S. population had a social network account as of 2018, according to Statista. That makes it likely that you will be able to locate your former antagonists via an online search.

Tracking down the people who hurt you and looking at them again may be emotionally challenging. The bullying interlude of your childhood may not have had a clean and distinct ending. There may never have been a time when you knew, with certainty, that the terror was over and you were safe. You may never have had closure.

There may be a part of you that believes you still have reason to fear your tormentors. You may believe that they would bully you again, if they were given a chance. Although you have likely acquired better coping skills now than you had as a child, you may be uncertain that you would be able to handle another round of abuse.

You might have lived your life in fear of running into the people who hurt you during your childhood. Perhaps you have envisioned an impromptu meeting with one of your abusers.

You might have imagined that you were at a restaurant, and the former bully walked in, recognized you, and launched into a repeat performance of what he or she did to you when you were children.

In your imagination, perhaps you were waiting in line at a supermarket, bank, or theatre. Or maybe you were on vacation, taking a walk, or on an airplane.

It's possible you catastrophized that the bully could somehow find a way to enter your present life, surprise you, and leave you defenseless. You might have experienced the scenario as if it had actually happened. It's possible that you already have anticipated the shock, horror, and fear you would experience if it actually happened. You might have convinced yourself that, however you responded to the reemergence of the bully, it would be wrong — again.

Maybe you have believed that running into the bully would be the worst thing that could ever happen to you. Perhaps you have been certain that seeing the faces of the people from your childhood would send you into a tailspin from which you could never recover.

You may see the internet as a threat, and your instinct may be to do everything possible to avoid connecting with your foes online. That may be the right thing for you to do, but avoidance probably will not help you recover from the trauma of childhood bullying. Also, it will not bring you any nearer than you are now to finding peace.

Cracking open the door to your past, and seeing where the people of your childhood are, can bring you a step closer to healing. The people you find online may surprise you. They probably little resemble the people you once knew. In fact, you most likely don't know anything about them. But that can change.

From the safety of your own space, which you control, you can find your foes online and learn whatever there is to be gleaned about them. You will be able to ascertain that they are mere mortals.

They are not larger than life. In fact, they are as human as you.

Seeing them as they really are, instead of as you may have imagined them to be, can help you put them into perspective. The mythology that you may have created for yourself about how they control your fate can dissipate.

These people, as adults, may have their good traits and their bad. Some of them may have acquired real-world power and wealth. Others may have earned respect and acclaim. Yet others may have crashed and burned, and when you find them online, you may see only shadows of the people you expected to find.

For the most part, their lives are probably as interesting, or as mundane, as the people you run into every day. The stories of their adult lives have probably been a mixed bag of good and bad, successes and failures, and sickness and health.

The differences between the random individuals who cross paths with you now and the bullies who have occupied your mind for so long are probably negligible. If you can handle meeting strangers in your daily life, then you may also be able to deal with these antagonists from your past with whom you no longer have any contact.

Finding your former classmates online does not have to lead to a confrontation such as the ones you may have imagined. Some of what you see may bewilder or amuse you.

Until you look for the people of your childhood, you can only guess at what you will discover. You may find yourself both pleasantly, and unpleasantly, surprised. Whatever you find, though, is better than contemplating the unknown day after day. Finding out anything about the people who caused you so much pain would probably be easier than living with no knowledge of them or blowing their importance all out of proportion in your imagination.

Facing your foes online can be terrifying. However, whatever you see, you can probably cope with. If you face the profiles of the people who once hurt you, they will likely lose their power to paralyze you.

They are only flesh and blood, after all. Seek them out, online, to prove that to yourself.

Begin to shrink the monsters in your mind down to a more manageable size. Perhaps, eventually, you will be able to banish them completely.

Beginning Your Search

The passage of time can change former classmates' appearances. People may marry and change their last names. They can move out of state or even out of the country.

They may end up anywhere, doing almost anything, with almost anybody. Nothing you find online should surprise you.

When you feel ready, get started. Use the search engine with which you are the most comfortable. Type in a name you remember. Many times, even when people change their names, they leave behind a digital trail that includes their former monikers.

You may turn up newspaper articles, Wikipedia entries, Amazon author page listings, IMDB celebrity pages ... or just about anything. These findings will not necessarily have anything to do with the people you are seeking — particularly, if the individual has a common name. In that case, you may want to add the state where you went to school to your search.

If your search engine of choice is Google, you can click on the "images" tab and see whether any photos of the person you're researching appear. Even though faces change over the years, you may be able to recognize the adult version of your former classmate.

Clicking on the photo that most resembles your classmate will probably lead you to a web page — an article, staff listing, blog, or the like — where you can discover additional information. A short biography may include social networking links. Use those clues to find the individual's social network profiles, and then hope that the person in question has been willing to share information on at least one social network with the public.

If you are a frequent user, you may feel at home with one or more of the major social networks. Do a search for a former tormentor within your favorite social network, just as you would search for anyone else.

You probably do that on a regular basis, anyway. Simply apply the search skills you already have to tracking down the people from your past.

Sometimes, as you may have discovered, it can be easier to find someone's social network profile from outside of the network itself. Type the person's name, the state where that individual once lived, and the name of the social network

158 · STACEY J. MILLER

(such as Facebook or LinkedIn) into a search engine, and see whether you can find the individual.

You may find several candidates — people who share the individual's name and have some association with the state where you went to school. To further narrow down your search, see whether you can check out the ages of the prospects.

Some social networks, such as LinkedIn, report back to account holders the identity of anyone who may have viewed their profile. You may feel unsafe knowing that your former classmates could be aware that you viewed their profiles, so it may be important to ensure they will not find out.

To maintain your privacy, you can search Facebook, LinkedIn — or any other site on the internet — by opening up an incognito window in Google Chrome or a private window in Safari. Other browsers, including Internet Explorer and Firefox, also have private search modes.

When a new window opens in your browser, you will be able to type a URL into the address bar. You can conduct your research, as you normally would, secure in the knowledge that the average person will not be able to trace the search back to you.

Going incognito while you track down the people from your past sets up a one-way mirror between them and you. While you can view your former tormentors, they will not know you are there.

They cannot know where you are or what you are doing. There would be no way for them to know that you are even thinking about them. You can be sure that you are not poking the bear when you search for your former tormentors while you are going incognito.

Searching the web covertly may sound slightly creepy. It may seem to you that you are cyber stalking people from the past. In fact, you are doing just the opposite. This is not about obsessing about those who once abused you. On the contrary: this is a way to stop focusing on them. Your purpose is to see them once more so that you can move on.

You are facing the people who once terrorized you so that you can see they no longer have any power over you. Information that the internet makes available will help you to reduce the real estate your former abusers take up in your mind. You're using the internet's power to find closure.

That doesn't mean you have to find every single one of those individuals who were involved in the bullying or that you have to track them all down at the same time. You can search for only the people you choose, and you can do it at a leisurely pace.

This doesn't have to consume much of your time. An internet search may take only a few minutes.

You may be interested in learning what you can about the antagonists of your childhood. But consider limiting the amount of energy you put into scratching that itch.

Suppressing the memories of what happened to you for so long might have been a helpful coping mechanism. Remembering the story of what happened to you might have been far more beneficial.

So far, so good. Facing the characters of your story online may be an important part of what you need to do to get past the trauma of your childhood. But, as you visit the past, keep in mind that you live in the present. Remind yourself of how far away from your current life these people are.

You may uncover interesting or unsettling information, and it's okay to let yourself be surprised. But don't get stuck. Life, and time, are finite. You have other productive things to do, and most of them are probably more constructive than dwelling on the people who once hurt you.

Search for Your Foes Online

Keep your eye on your purpose, which is to find your foes online before they can ambush you. Travel into the past online, because you may find it helpful. But remember how great it will feel to return to the present.

Most people from your childhood are probably are just a few clicks away. Perhaps you will look up a couple of them and be more than ready to move on. Facing just one or two of those monsters online may help you put them all into their rightful perspective.

If you track down only one person, though, you'll almost certainly want to choose the individual who mattered the most: the bully.

Finding the Bully Online

Finding the bully of your childhood will probably be a quick process once you begin to search. In fact, you may even find the bully too quickly.

Between the time you decide to take the plunge and the moment when you are face-to-face with the former bully's social network profile, only a few moments may elapse. Once you enter the name and a few details into the search engine box, a link to the bully's virtual self may emerge right away.

One more click could take you to this person's social network page or another site that contains his or her profile — including at least one current photograph.

Be prepared. When you have tracked down the bully online, you may feel almost as distraught as if you are meeting this individual in person again. Seeing the bully's virtual presence may trick your mind into thinking it is a real-world meeting. You may flash back to the terror and shame you felt as a child. In an instant, you may feel vulnerable and threatened as if no time had passed.

Reassure yourself that there is no need to be afraid. You are sitting safely behind a computer, tablet, or smart phone. The bully's profile — not the actual person, but only a digital representation — is contained inside a screen or monitor. The pixels you see have no power to hurt you. The bully is not in the room with you. He or she cannot do anything to hurt you, take anything from you, or ask anything of you. You do not have to demand anything of yourself, either. Keep reminding yourself that you are safe.

If you choose to read about the bully, and you want to look at any images that might be associated with that individual, then you can do so at your own pace. You can see as much, or as little, as you'd like.

Viewing the profile most likely will show you how the years have changed the bully. This is not the boy or girl who once abused you. This is an adult. Hopefully, this person has matured. Maybe he or she has mellowed. The passage of years, hopefully, has had a positive effect on the bully.

Likely, the individual has become a responsible citizen and is leading an ordinary, and perhaps mundane, life. He or she probably poses no threat to society, generally, or to you, specifically. You are in no danger.

As you will undoubtedly see from viewing the bully's profile, you are nowhere on his or her radar. The bully's life has gone on, and you have not been a part of it.

This person may not have thought about you in years. It is possible that, once your paths diverged, the bully never thought of you again.

Memories of the bully may have stayed with you. However, that may not have been mutual. The bully may not remember a whole lot about you.

Maybe, to this person, hurting children was such a trivial matter that it didn't merit further consideration. Once it was over, that was the end of it. In that case, you may be virtually looking at someone who has no clue that you have put any energy at all into thinking about your past relationship. It is possible that this person bullied so many other children besides you that the specifics of torturing any particular individual could not remain.

On the other hand, maybe as the bully matured, the memories of hurting children became too painful to bear. Maybe, as an adult, this person didn't want to think of himself or herself as a former bully. It is possible that your former abuser has purposely or involuntarily blocked all memories of that time.

Or maybe this person does remember you. Maybe you are looking at the profile of someone who always regretted bullying you. Perhaps this individual has spent time wondering what had become of you and hoping that, somehow, you had found a way to enjoy health, success, and happiness.

You cannot determine all those things by looking at the bully's online presence. But you can see the information this person has made available to the public.

It is possible that you can discover the location of this individual's home or workplace. You also may be able to learn what he or she does for a living; whether the bully ever married or had children; what this individual cares about; and how this person spends recreational time.

You may even be able to fill in the blanks between the time that you intersected with the bully and the present. Through the person's online profile, you may learn which other schools the bully attended; places the person has lived; and companies for which he or she has worked.

A Facebook profile, in particular, can offer opportunities to unravel quite a bit of information about the bully's life. It may be possible to find out whether the bully has recently visited a beach, walked a dog, visited a doctor, or seen a sunset. You may learn what the bully ate for breakfast or drank with dinner. Perhaps you will see what the bully thinks about, hopes for, and fears.

This information may not be earth-shattering to you. As a matter of fact, you probably don't care about any of it.

The details of the bully's current life shouldn't matter to you. What may be of interest is the fact that none of it involves you or represents any sort of threat to you.

The less you care about what you see, the better off you are. You can probably feel the monster shrink a little bit more with every second you spend viewing the minutiae of the bully's days and nights.

Despite what you might have imagined as a child, the bully probably hasn't taken the world by storm. He or she most likely controls very little. Certainly, the former bully no longer has any power over you.

On the other hand, maybe the bully has been quite successful in life. It is possible that he or she has done well professionally, personally, or socially.

Perhaps this person is now a business owner or a community leader. It is possible the person who once bullied you is working to find a cure for cancer, lobbying for animals' rights, caring for aging parents or grandparents, raising children or grandchildren, or making contributions to society in ways that you could appreciate.

From a distance, the former bully may look like a decent, hardworking individual who is caring, funny, or kind. That may be interesting for you to note. Maybe, if things had been different, the adult you're seeing online could be someone you would admire.

Or you may feel nothing except loathing. That is also okay; you are allowed to feel anger toward someone who derailed your childhood. You are not required to be a saint.

Acknowledge what you are feeling in response to what you find in the bully's profile, and make no demands on yourself. You do not have to feel any particular way about it.

To satisfy your curiosity, you may want to learn whether the individual stayed in touch with any of your former classmates. You may be able to find this out on Facebook, if his or her friends list is public. In the bully's photo albums, you may see pictures of recent get-togethers that include images of those individuals. Some of those photos may be tagged with names you recognize.

The world wide web is called that for a reason. Checking out the bully's online presence can lead to opportunities to virtually see former mutual acquaintances. Go there, if you'd like. Shrink the monsters all in one sitting.

Or stay focused only on the bully for awhile. Look at the images that are available. You may see wedding pictures, casual shots, or corporate photos. In them, you may see something familiar about the face or posture of the person who once hurt you.

Perhaps, since so much time has elapsed, you'll feel nothing at all when you look at that bully's image. What you see, perhaps, will be anticlimactic. You may have imagined an encounter with the bully for so long that, even though you've turned it into a type of reality thanks to the internet, it is still hard to believe that it is taking place.

Don't be surprised if looking at the online presence of the bully who has haunted your nightmares underwhelms you, and you feel very little.

No one can require you to respond in any particular way, and nobody has the right to expect any specific reaction from you. There is no proper or incorrect response to what you find.

It is possible that you will surprise yourself by reacting more emotionally than you expected. Perhaps your virtual visit with the bully will surprise you by unleashing a torrent of fresh pain.

Maybe you will grieve because you never received satisfaction or justice. This person never paid a price for causing you pain. You may resent the fact that the bully is smiling while you are hurting, and the bully has achieved success and happiness while you have been stuck in a place of regret, fear, and self-recrimination.

166 · STACEY J. MILLER

There are legitimate reasons for you to feel all of what you're feeling. If you are overcome with fury that the bully's life has fully gone on in some ways that yours has not, allow yourself to express it safely.

Tap into your coping toolbox, and pull out the best of the strategies you have. They might involve taking deep, calming breaths; meditating; practicing yoga poses; immersing yourself in nature or art; escaping into a book, film, or TV program; creating something; hugging someone; connecting with a friend; volunteering; committing a random act of kindness; cleaning; going to the gym; walking or running; doing physical labor; treating yourself to something that brings you pleasure; or even just playing with your dog, gazing at your goldfish, or snuggling with your cat.

Do what you need to do to take care of yourself. Expect that you will be able to work through your response to encountering the monster of your childhood online and resolve any issues that arise from the experience.

However, if you need help in handling your emotions, please reach out for it. Make sure that you do not feel alone. Understand that leaning on others for support is an act of strength rather than an admission of weakness.

As you recall the events that created the trauma, realize how far away they were — in time, and maybe also in geography — from where you are now.

This person hurt you once. But that is over. He or she no longer has to matter to you, nor does the bully have to occupy any more of your energy. Life has moved on for both of you.

Maybe, finally, you can let this person go.

Finding the Bully's Court Online

If you've already found the bully online, you have probably realized that he or she isn't omnipotent. The grownup version of the bully isn't the child you remembered, nor has that individual evolved into the superhuman you may envisioned.

Your research has almost certainly turned up the fact that the former bully is just a regular person who has no thoughts about you and no hold over you. If you already have seen that for yourself, then moving forward to the next part of the process — tracking down the other abusers of your childhood — should be even easier.

However, you may have decided not to begin by finding the bully online. Maybe you don't feel ready for that. Facing the biggest monster of them all may not be the best place for you to begin. You may prefer to take smaller steps toward reaching that goal.

You know what feels right to you. The choice of whether to move ahead in tracking down the bully, as well as the timing of that effort, is yours.

Your path forward may meander, and you may even take a few step backwards at times. That's okay. You are still traversing the road that leads to healing rather than standing still.

For now, it may be wiser to consider facing the individuals whose abuse was almost, but not quite, as intense as the bully's. The members of the bully's court — the bully's closest allies — hurt you nearly as much. They may be taking up far more space in your head than they are worth, and you can reclaim that emotional real estate, too.

The members of the bully's court were the bully's closest allies at one time. When the bully hurt you, these were among the most enthusiastic cheerleaders. These were the individuals who picked up the slack and tormented you almost as skillfully as the bully when their leader wasn't around to abuse you. Their behavior may have been as egregious as that of the bully.

In fact, it may be difficult for you to imagine the bully without also visualizing those closest to that individual. Those who encouraged the bully, and responded appreciatively to the abuse you experienced, exponentially worsened your suffering.

They ranked high in the social order of the class and held enough power so that, if they had chosen to, they could have changed everything for you. If they had stood up to the bully, they might have ended your suffering.

Because they had access to the bully, they might have been able to convince him or her to stop hurting you. It might have been possible for them to shift the focus away from you and toward a group activity that wouldn't have hurt anybody.

Doing the right thing might have meant taking a risk, but the rewards would have been immeasurable — for themselves, and for you. They would have been doing something decent, and they might have felt better about themselves.

If they had earned the right to be proud of their actions, they might have been heroes in the eyes of others, too. They might have earned the respect of the school community through their courage and willingness to stand up for what was right.

Instead, they were sycophants who chose to score points with their leader and gain admiration from those further down the social ladder. The bully's court could have abandoned the bully any time they wanted. Instead, they piled on and attacked you. They had a choice to make, and they picked the wrong one.

You do not have to forgive them, and you don't have to wish them well. It isn't your responsibility to try to understand why they did what they did or how they could have lived with their decision to do it.

But it may be time to begin to let go of asking questions about their motives. That will help release the power the members of the bully's court have held over you.

It may be time to face the bully's court members online and reduce them to their actual size. Seeing what has become of them in the adult world can go a long way toward accomplishing that.

You probably remember the names and faces of the bully's court members. Use the same research methods that led you to the bully to track down the members of the bully's inner circle.

As you're looking, don't be thrown off if a person with the right name seems to live in the wrong state or even the wrong country. Expect the unexpected. People relocate, for example.

If you are dismissing the possibility that you have found the right individual because the spouses' or children's names, or the photos associated with the individual's profile, seem incongruous, slow down and think it through more carefully.

The person you are seeking may have married someone of a different ethnicity or an unexpected gender, and may have taken his (or her) last name. The children may have inherited the features of a relative whose genetic legacy would surprise you. The person you are seeking may be raising children of whom he or she is not the biological parents. Don't rush past the person you're seeking because of your judgments and expectations.

Members of the bully's court may have professions you couldn't have imagined. Given their popularity and the seemingly limitless potential they had as children, you might have assumed they would grow up to become supermodels or jet setters, play professional sports, manage a Fortune 500 company, or would at least have married rich enough to pay for plastic surgery that would keep them looking 21 years old forever.

Instead, they may have become unremarkable people who are not necessarily rich, successful, glamorous, or beautiful. They may not have thousands of social media friends and followers. They may not own multiple luxury homes, yachts, and private islands.

You may find, by looking at their photos, that they are overweight or underweight. Their hairline may have receded, and their muscles may have turned to flab. There may be few signs that these were the young people who once held the tickets to the school's most admired clique.

Now, they may hold ordinary jobs. They may lead unimpressive lives. Perhaps they have long since given up pursuing what everyone at school believed they were entitled to attain.

They may have peaked in popularity, ambition, and success when they were children. Since then, they may have lost their ability to charm and achieve. Perhaps their stature has plummeted.

Their approval may have fallen in value or become universally worthless. They may have surrendered their ability to make anyone feel good, bad, or anything at all.

Looking at their social profiles may drive the point home that anything they once thought of you, or said about you, is irrelevant now. The members of the bully's inner circle do not own the world. They occupy only one small corner of it.

On the other hand, maybe certain members of the bully's court have done well. Maybe they have found peace, happiness, or financial success. Their contentment probably means they have not reached into the past and given you much thought at all. Certainly, if the reason they hurt you was because they were feeling insecure or frustrated, then their present-day satisfaction is a win for you, too. You don't have to worry that someone who is in a good place emotionally, professionally, and socially is still looking for scapegoats for their misery.

This person probably just wants to forget his or her past transgressions and enjoy the pleasures available in his or her present-day moments. You don't have to lose sleep over someone who is doing well, nor do you have to waste any more of your waking time dwelling on what they did and pondering why they did it.

Check out what happened to the bully's closest associates, and satisfy your curiosity. Then you will be able to move on without the weight of worrying about people who no longer matter.

Finding the Followers Online

You may choose not to begin your search with the bully or members of the bully's court. You may, instead, try to find someone from your class who was less threatening to you — say, a follower.

There probably were many people who followed the class leaders in tormenting you. You may remember their abuse as clearly as you remember the bullying by those higher up in the chain of command. However, although the bully's name and face, and the names and faces of the bully's court members, are probably indelibly stamped on your memory, you may only partially remember some of the others. The passage of time might have dimmed or jumbled the rest.

Some of the followers may stand out in your mind clearly, though. These are likely the people who supported the bully and the members of the bully's court with the most enthusiasm. Maybe they seemed more self-confident than the other people who were part of the tribe, and maybe they appeared to be enjoying themselves the most of all the followers.

These are probably the people who made it their business to ensure that the tormenting continued even if the bullies or their closest associates took a day off or became temporarily distracted.

While some followers may have found a different way to use their time when there were few A-listers around to impress, these other followers were eager to abuse you, anyway. You probably have put them into their own special category of tormentors: vicious, weak people who lacked the initiative to find a productive way to spend their time and had to borrow the worst of the class leaders' ideas.

These followers probably are stuck in your mind because their behavior disgusted you so deeply. As loathsome as these followers were, they still may be easier for you to face than those higher up the social ladder. Therefore, you may choose to find one of these followers first — ideally, an individual whose name and childhood face you can fully remember.

Facebook is probably a good starting point for your search. See whether you can find this person's profile. Even people — women *and* men (keep an open mind to the possibilities) — who changed their last names when they were married frequently cite their maiden names, too, on their social network profiles.

You may find multiple people by the name you remember. A maiden name may turn up as a middle name, so consider individuals who have a different last name from the one you remember if the first and middle names resonate with you. Check out their profile pictures, and see whether you can find one whose image might be a match for the individual you remember.

However, since years have passed, identifying the follower visually may be challenging. Also, many people choose photos of their children, pets, or other images instead of their own as their profile photo, at least on a temporary basis.

You may have to click on the hyperlinked names of more than one person to find the individual you are seeking. When you get to someone's page, check for clues, including the individual's place of residence. He or she may, or may not, still be living in the state where you attended school. You will see only the details and photos that the individuals have made public.

If the person's photo album is available to the public, you may want to click through it. You may find recognizable names, and faces, in the photo album if the follower has kept in touch with former classmates through the social media.

Even if the follower has not stayed in touch with the students you mutually knew, you may find vintage, or throwback, photos of other classmates that were taken at about the time when you were in school together. You may find team pictures that can be enlarged to reveal the faces of people you remember at the time when you knew them.

Some of those images may be painful for you to see. They may remind you of a past filled with good times for your classmates, and isolation and despair for you.

The bully, or members of the bully's court, may turn up in the follower's photo album. Be prepared for that. You may also see photos of some of the silent bystanders of your class — people who saw everything and refused to intervene on your behalf.

One connection can lead to others. If you click on the individual's "friends" page, you may find hyperlinks to other people whose names and images you recognize. You have no obligation to click on any of them, but you can. It is in your hands. You can drill down as deeply as you want and continue the process.

The followers, today, probably are very different people from the ones you recall. Maybe it will ease your mind to see where they are and what they are doing.

Click on their "about" pages. If the information is available to the public, you may learn what the followers did after the time when your paths intersected. You may find out whether the followers continued school, got married, became parents, found employment, became active in their communities, developed hobbies, and the like.

If you read about their personal and professional lives, you'll be able to learn what matters to them. You may find that you have certain things in common with them.

See who they are. Humanize them.

They behaved horribly to you during your childhood, and you do not have to forget that. But you can eliminate the need to worry that they will ever hurt you again.

Fill the vacated space in your mind with people about whom you care, pursuits that matter to you, adventures that excite you, knowledge or skills you would like to acquire, goals you want to accomplish, memories you cherish, and works of art you would like to see or create. Hope, satisfaction, health, and joy can replace the darkness.

Finding the Silent Bystanders Online

In this era of zero tolerance for bullying, many schools have programs in place to teach students what they should do if they see children tormenting others. Ideally, they will not just stand by and watch. They will tell an adult about it, or they will encourage a child who is being targeted by bullies to report the problematic behaviors.

They will know that bullying is unacceptable and can have serious consequences for everyone. They will have heard that standing up to bullies is often enough to convince them to back down. Therefore, children today may decide to short-circuit bullying when they see it by confronting the tormentors and telling them to stop. Whatever students with this type of training decide to do when they spot bullying behaviors, they likely will find support for their choice as long as they do not just stand by and watch it.

But during the childhood you shared with the silent members of your class, few schools took the problem of bullying seriously. The students who stood by and watched wordlessly while others were hurting you were part of a different culture — one that endorsed secrecy in the face of bullying.

176 · STACEY J. MILLER

Back then, it is likely that no one labeled bullying behaviors. Nobody acknowledged the problem, and no one discussed what to do when it arose. Therefore, the silent bystanders of the class may not have known the best way to handle bullying or even that they were supposed to get involved.

You don't have to excuse the fact that they stood by, watching, as others hurt you. They still could have chosen to do the right thing, even if no one told them they had that option.

Even children who aren't specifically taught the difference between right and wrong may be capable of figuring it out for themselves. Certainly, when children saw that you were being hurt, they might have empathized. They could have stepped in and defended you, just as they would have wanted somebody to defend them.

They might have expressed anger at the abusers and demanded that they stop tormenting you. It wouldn't have required any special coaching to speak up for you.

If they had refused to tolerate the bullying behavior, they would have been your heroes. You might remember them as the people who saved you from years of suffering.

Had the situation been reversed, and other people were targeted by bullies, you might have chosen to not remain silent. Even though it was a different time, there was still a right and a wrong response. You might have chosen to use your voice to put a stop to bullying.

Yes, the culture has changed, but staying silent while a child was being hurt was never okay. It was always indefensible, from the target's point of view.

You know that, and it hurts to think those who remained silent while you were being tortured got away with their behavior. It may infuriate you.

Or you may recognize that, even if the silent bystanders wanted to help you, they might have been too afraid. You may understand that watching an innocent classmate being bullied was also a painful experience for them and that those who chose silence over action also suffered. They might have experienced feelings of guilt, sadness, frustration, and helplessness. Their choices may have created long-lasting negative consequences for them, too.

Perhaps, too, the bullying they watched you experience was only a small part of their world. They were real children with their own lives and their own problems. The silent bystanders starred in their dramas, and faced their own challenges, just as you did. They may have suffered in ways that you didn't know about at the time and of which you are still unaware.

It's impossible to be sure, because they never told you how they were living. Therefore, you had no way to understand how they were feeling.

You do, however, remember the bullying activities in which they did not participate. You recall the taunts they didn't hurl at you, the threats they didn't make, and the violence they didn't perpetrate.

It would have been easier for the silent bystanders to join the tormentors than to abstain. Bullying you may have been an easy way to gain acceptance from their peers and, possibly, advance a rung or two up the social ladder of the classroom.

They didn't do that. Instead, they resisted the temptation to actively hurt you and enjoy the possible rewards of doing so.

They had a moral code to which they adhered, inadequate though it might have seemed to you.

But they did remain neutral. While they didn't help you, they didn't make things worse, either. That might have been the best they were capable of doing.

As you think about the silent bystanders online, shift your focus to what they didn't do rather than what they did. You may find yourself able to feel gratitude.

Find some of the silent members of your class online. You don't have to find them all.

Looking at the social network profiles of a sampling of the classmates who were silent may be sufficient. Check out the social media posts of those silent classmates who have made them available to the public.

Hear what these former silent classmates now have to say. Maybe, now, they are passionate about the things that matter to them.

Their posts may indicate that they are vocal about politics, human or animal rights, or protecting the planet. Maybe they have initiated campaigns to raise funds for a worthy cause, or maybe they have signed petitions to achieve positive change.

Possibly, the formerly silent bystanders of your class are now communicative, and they are aggressively pursuing justice. It would have been better for you — and, undoubtedly, for them — if they had chosen to behave that way during your shared childhoods.

You can regret the fact that they were not heroes years ago while, potentially, appreciating where they are now. Perhaps your mutual past, and the mistakes they made then, provided motivation for them to evolve into kinder, more benevolent human beings.

Maybe their social network profiles show that they still are keeping their opinions and their thoughts to themselves. They may be private people who have never found the courage, or the passion, to articulate or pursue much of anything. That shouldn't surprise you, given what you remember about the children they used to be. Perhaps they have always found it easier to stay quiet and compliant to get along. Taking the path of least resistance may have been their life-long habit.

In any case, it is unnecessary for you to judge them in the present or change your feelings about who they were in the past. They were wrong to allow others to bully you. You have a right to hold them accountable for the choices they made.

They acted the way most students did at the time and for many of the same reasons. They weren't directed to do otherwise, and they lacked the instincts and skills to do better. Maybe that is just the type of people they were born to be.

Remember who the silent bystanders were, but focus on who they are now. Hope that, if they remember you at all, they feel remorseful for doing nothing to help you. Trust that, if they have their own children, or if they are responsible for others' kids, they have taught them to make better choices than they once did.

They may teach others to be stronger and better by sharing the mistakes they made. Perhaps they are leading, and they have led, through their example of what not to do.

Believe they are sorry. Know that what they didn't do during your childhood was a reflection of who they were, at the time, and not a judgment about you.

Finding the Converts Online

It was one thing to be abused or ignored by people you scarcely knew. That was horrible enough. When a former friend joined in and attacked you, that might have felt exponentially worse than when others did it.

A convert was someone you once trusted. You cared about this person, and you believed he or she reciprocated your feelings.

When the friend joined the tribe of people who were suctioning the joy out of your life, then he or she became part of the problem. This person's defection hurt you personally in a way that a stranger's abuse never could.

The convert may have been someone who had been your friend when you were younger. He or she may have been in your classes at a time when things were better for you.

Or this may have been a person you had recently met and who, at first, befriended you. Later, when sentiment turned against you and everyone else in the class started their abusive behavior, this former friend may have joined in.

This person, and anyone else who was converted by the bullies, betrayed your friendship and damaged your trust. That was just unspeakably wrong.

Your former friends should have supported you when you needed them. They should have been as horrified as you were by the abuse that you were experiencing, and they should have done everything in their power to stop it.

People who cared about you shouldn't have given in to the temptation to gain popularity by supporting the bullies. They shouldn't have tried to climb the social ladder by stepping on you.

Former friends shouldn't have ignored your need for at least one supporter. They shouldn't have walked away from someone who needed an ally. They let you down badly.

You can think about all of that as you look at their social profiles. You can ruminate about how, where, when, and why they hurt you. Or you can focus, instead, on the friendship you once enjoyed together.

You can click through old pictures in the converts' photo albums. It's possible that you were nearby when some of them were taken. Maybe seeing the younger versions of the converts will elicit pleasant memories.

Maybe, just for a while, you can think about the good times you shared. You can remember why you cared about these people and why they once mattered to you.

You can indulge in remembering what you once meant to them. Maybe you can remember nicknames you had for each other, confidences you exchanged, or memories you shared that no one else knew about.

Perhaps you can recall why you once considered these people your friends. They might have had some special qualities that attracted you. Perhaps your friendship was so intense that you believed it would last forever.

For their part, these converts might have intended to be your friends for life. The events that occurred might have surprised them as much as they blindsided you.

Your former friends might have chosen sides against you in shock, panic, or confusion. Maybe they were taken by surprise every bit as much as you were. They might have worried that, if they stayed by your side, the bullies would target them, too — and they might have believed they couldn't have handled that and didn't even want to try.

Perhaps, even as they were betraying you, they understood what that were sacrificing. Maybe they felt as horrible as you did about their choice. It could be they were fully conscious of what they were doing, and they hated their behavior, too.

Maybe, as you view the converts' social profiles, you can tap into your best self to send your former friends appreciation for all they once meant to you. You may even be able to hope they were able to forgive themselves for causing you so much pain. If that isn't your choice, that's also okay.

They gained the upper hand in your relationship for a time, but that was long ago. At this point, you are on equal terms again. How you respond to the memories of your former friends is up to you.

Finding the Other Targets Online

If you were the loser of your class, you probably weren't the only one. There might have been other children who were also tormented.

Although the other targets and you had something in common, your mutual misfortune and pain might have kept you apart. You might have feared consoling each other would worsen your own positions.

Perhaps you refused to admit that you had anything in common with those losers. In their isolation, they might have struck you as troubled, unpalatable outsiders. You might have shunned them just as others were avoiding you.

Perhaps you felt too powerless to help them. You couldn't even help yourself.

You might even have found temporary relief during the times when your classmates were focusing their negative attention and directing their bad behavior on someone besides you. While they were abusing other targets, they weren't torturing you. Perhaps they could only focus on one person at a time, and their outrageous behavior toward their other targets provided you with a short reprieve. Maybe you secretly felt relieved during those times when it was someone else's turn.

The other targets also might have looked forward to the times when the bullies' attention was on you instead of on them. They might have exhaled when you were the target while they were temporarily in the clear.

Bullying fosters an "us against them" mentality. You may blame yourself for your refusal, or your inability, to help other targets. It may be difficult to accept the fact that you didn't help others when they were suffering. Perhaps it dismays you to remember that you weren't able, or willing, to transcend the gap between the other targets and you, given all that you had in common.

It may bewilder you to remember that you were as disgusted by the targets as your other classmates were by you. It may confuse you that you were capable of rejecting others at a time when you were so hurt by rejection yourself.

You could have at least tried to make things easier for other targets, because you knew how it felt when nobody reached out to help you. Perhaps you wish you had handled things differently. Maybe, somehow, you could have done better.

Tracking down the other targets' social network profiles may help you discover that they came through the other side of the experience, just as you did. They survived. Maybe they thrived.

184 · STACEY J. MILLER

Most likely, they went on to enjoy an array of rich experiences. They may have surrounded themselves with wonderful, caring people. Check out their status updates to see whether you can find any news to celebrate with them from your side of the one-way mirror. At least, what you find may allay your fears that you helped to cause irreparable harm to people who didn't deserve it.

Forgive yourself for doing the best you could to survive a horrible situation. Okay, so you didn't earn sainthood. Generally, children do not ... and you were surrounded by people who were behaving terribly. The dismal environment in which you found yourself undoubtedly contributed to the poor decisions that you made.

Remember, too, that you weren't taught how to confront bullies, either. Back then, nobody was. The fact that you were targeted by bullies didn't automatically make you an expert.

You may be able to release your feelings of guilt for your behavior. At the same time, maybe you can send understanding to the other targets who made similar hurtful choices for many of the same reasons.

Finding the Teachers and Coaches Online

Teachers and coaches were paid to do a few things, but perhaps the most important of them all was to keep the children in their care safe. Abandoning that responsibility should never have been an option.

Not everyone has the skills or talent to work with children. As a student, you might have run into teachers or coaches who were incompetent, lazy, frustrated with their responsibilities, dissatisfied with their compensation or social status, or just plain burned out. Perhaps they were even sadistic enough to torment you themselves.

It was dishonorable for teachers and coaches who didn't belong in their positions to collect paychecks they hadn't earned. The fact that they failed to protect you, and that they may even have participated in abusing you, was a travesty.

The teachers and coaches who let you down shouldn't have been in a position of responsibility that involved children. Those jobs were too important to be filled by people who were unworthy, or who lacked the talent or skills to succeed.

Teaching and coaching is a privilege. Some people were born to do it, and they can turn education into a joy. They can model kindness and help students learn to work as a team. Others should not be allowed anywhere near children, particularly when some of those students are experiencing serious problems.

It was unfortunate that you encountered adults who should have chosen different professions. On top of that, it was terrible that their incompetence and errors of judgment caused you harm.

But you, too, might have made missteps on your way to finding the best possible job. When you were in your late teens and early twenties, and it was time to enter the adult workforce, you might not have chosen the right approach to beginning your career, either. You might have swung and missed a few times. It might have taken you awhile to find out where you fit into the working world.

If you made mistakes professionally, then perhaps you can empathize with teachers and coaches who also messed up. It is possible you were even partly responsible for helping the teachers and coaches of your past decide to redirect their en-

186 · STACEY J. MILLER

ergies. Maybe seeing your pain, and realizing that they could do nothing to alleviate it — and, perhaps, seeing that they were only adding to it — inspired them to find a career better suited to their temperaments and energies.

Check out the social network profiles of the teachers and coaches who let you down most memorably. Perhaps they are now retired, or maybe they have switched careers. Maybe they became productive doing something else, far away from the classroom, gym, or playing field. Perhaps they still are ashamed of their job performance as teachers and coaches, and they wish they could remedy their mistakes.

There's nothing they can do to change the past, but you can find satisfaction in seeing that the worst teachers and coaches are no longer in a position to harm other students. You may be able to find relief in knowing for certain that other children are now safe from them.

Finding the Administrators Online

Although teachers and coaches may have had autonomy in the classroom and gym, and on the playing field, they answered to the school administrators. The principal or headmaster ran the school and had ultimate authority over everyone who worked there. Counselors were responsible for ensuring the children in their care received the education and care to which they were entitled.

If the school was unsafe for even one of the children who attended, and it was unable to provide that student with what the taxpayers (or their parents, if this was a private institution) were paying for, then the administrators weren't doing their jobs.

While teachers might have been young and incapable of handling some of the challenges that came their way, you had a right to expect administrators to be older, wiser, more experienced, and better trained. You had reason to believe they had earned their positions of authority and responsibility.

They were the adults who were in charge of everyone. Their focus, choices, and policies allowed children in their care to be bullied. They either actively enabled it or passively permitted it. In either case, what they did was wholly unacceptable.

You might have approached these administrators for help while you were in their care, or your parents (or possibly a teacher or another student) might have done that on your behalf. Perhaps the administrators did nothing because they didn't know what to do. They might have expressed anger because your problems were a nuisance for them and made them look bad in the eyes of others.

Perhaps they felt vulnerable. They might have worried that, if you were hurt on their watch, they could be held responsible.

In any case, these administrators held the power in your school, and they could have used it for good. Instead, they chose to ignore their potential for making a positive difference in your life. Through some combination of their incompetence, laziness, and selfishness, they might have made things even worse for you.

They might have let you down more than anyone else. Your greatest disappointment and your most intense fury may be aimed at the school administrators who failed you.

Brace yourself, and see whether you can find these administrators online. Along with social networks, check newspaper archives. You may learn whether the school administrators who were responsible for much of your suffering are still in charge of the school where you were abused, have moved onto the same job in another district, have advanced to an even more prestigious job, or have retired. Maybe you will learn they are now enthusiastically pursuing careers that bring them into contact with no children or anyone else over whom they have even the slightest bit of power.

What you find may bring you relief. Or what you learn may motivate you to keep a watchful eye on the policies governing bullying in any schools over which the administrators still have authority.

You can ensure that the school's policies are in compliance with state laws and regulations. Check out the school's anti-bullying policies which should be available online. If you can't find easily find them online, call or email the school to request them.

Go to the government's web site, www.stopbullying.gov. Under "Resources," click on "Laws & Policies." You will find state listings that will provide you with the facts about what schools must do to prevent, and confront, bullying and cyber bullying.

Be a watchdog. Exercise your right to attend community meetings and, if necessary, speak out about problems that you see in their anti-bullying policies. Make sure that the administrators who let you down will no longer be allowed to put another child in harm's way.

Finding Your Family Online

You may not need to find your family members online. Perhaps you have remained close and are in touch with them on a regular basis, in person or via phone, email, or text. Maybe you get together with your family for Thanksgiving dinners, or maybe you choose to never see them at all.

Some families can be wonderful. There actually are clans who appear to have stepped right out of a television sitcom. If you're lucky enough to be a member of that type of family, celebrate your good fortune. Don't ever take it for granted.

However, some families are dysfunctional or have cracks in their foundations. Some relationships within families just don't work. They can be toxic for reasons that are related to the childhood bullying you experienced. In those cases, keeping specific relatives at arm's length may be the wisest and most healthful path for everyone concerned.

Maybe, during your childhood, your family ferreted out the secret of your bullying and did their best to support you as they helped bring your nightmare to a conclusion. Perhaps they succeeded in guiding you past the dangers of the school where you were tormented and into a kinder, gentler, safer place.

Your family members might have realized they couldn't be with you all the time and keep you safe from everyone who might want to hurt you. They might have concluded it was, therefore, better to back off and let you learn to handle the bullying by yourself. Maybe you believe your family abandoned you when they should have helped.

Or perhaps your family knew nothing about the bullying you endured at school during your childhood. You might have hidden it from them, and they might not have figured it out for themselves. Perhaps you never forgave your family members for their lack of insight, and you attributed it to their failure to sufficiently care about you.

Maybe you were one of the rare children who took your family members into your confidence. It's possible they tried everything they could think of to help you, and they didn't succeed.

If you were the first person in your family to be targeted by bullies, or you were the only one who couldn't simply glide through the experience unscathed, they might not have known how to help you. They might have turned to other parents whose advice was inadequate.

Perhaps they approached teachers, coaches, and school administrators on your behalf and, somehow, managed to make things even worse. Maybe you suffered retribution because of your families' attempts to fix things for you.

Or maybe one or more family members groomed you to be a bully's target even before you entered a school for the first time. A parent, sibling, or another member of your family might have been the first bully in your life.

Perhaps, unintentionally, they let other people who were close to your family hurt you. Or, maybe, they knew that others were hurting you and did nothing to stop it. Possibly, their childhoods were tainted by abuse from family members or friends of the family, and maybe they never fixed what went wrong in their own lives. It's possible you were the recipient of the damage they suffered as children and were never able to resolve.

If your family members were so caring that they could have stepped out of the pages of a book by Laura Ingalls Wilder, then click on their social profiles and give each of them a virtual hug. Bask in the gratitude that you feel for them.

But, if that isn't the case, you are not alone.

Maybe, while you're sitting on the other side of your desktop, laptop, tablet, or cell phone, you can send your family members love, even if they were imperfect. Perhaps you can open yourself up to the love they are sending you — or would send to you, if they were able.

Finding Your Salvation Online

Now comes your reward for finding online all of the hurtful, nefarious characters in the story of your childhood bullying at school. You get to look up the people who were your heroes.

It would be great if the people who supported you, stuck their necks out for you, or tried to intervene for you had big, beautiful social network profiles that you could immediately find.

If they don't, then work even harder to locate them. This will be a pleasure, not a chore.

Updating yourself on the lives of the angels you encountered at school is the most wonderful part of the healing process. This is the part of the program where you can allow yourself to feel gratitude toward those who risked the wrath of the bullies, regardless of the potential consequences, and gave you the best they had to offer.

Look up the students who went out of their way to stand up for you. While you're online, see whether you can find some of the teachers and coaches who excelled at their jobs and cared about their students, too.

Find as many people as you can locate whose presence in your life mattered so much to you during such a difficult time. You've found your tormentors, and you have had the courage to revisit the pain they caused you. Now devote twice that amount of energy to finding, and virtually experiencing, the people who were the salvation of your childhood.

Bathe yourself in appreciation for the people who remembered you were human, cared about you, included you in their lives, and extended simple decency to you. Enjoy seeing the best of the people who populated the tough time of your childhood — other students and adults — and remembering how much their goodness affected you then.

If saviors were in short supply during the worst time in your childhood, then treat yourself to finding heroes from other periods of your past. Look up the students, teachers, coaches, friends, neighbors, colleagues, and others who gave you the gifts of respect and compassion.

Feel their goodness one more time. Bask in gratitude for their presence in your life. Immerse yourself in their love and light, and reflect it back to them.

While you're online, indulge in looking up other people who have acted selflessly and heroically. You don't have to know them personally. It isn't even necessary that you've ever heard of them.

Search the internet for "good news," and you'll find inspirational stories filled with great individuals and ordinary people who have done extraordinary things.

You will find that regular people can do heroic things when the situation calls for it. Cast around for evidence of decency and heroism, and you will find plenty. Be grateful for all of it. If you're inclined toward spirituality, meditate on the goodness that exists in the world. Send a prayer of thanks to your higher power, if that's a good fit for you.

Finding Bad News Online

When you search online for your foes, you probably expect to find most of them alive and functioning fairly well at ... something. However, in some cases, the truth may lie elsewhere. Search engines may provide links to news stories of arrests and convictions instead of active social network profiles. You may also find links to obituaries.

Former classmates, teachers, coaches, and administrators may post these stories on the timelines of their own social profiles. Such links may take you by surprise.

Learning that someone who hurt you has met with misfortune may seem like cosmic justice. Perhaps you will feel as if karma has undertaken the task of settling the score for you. You may feel relieved that a threat to you, and maybe to others, has been neutralized.

Perhaps you will print out news stories that can provide you with closure. In fact, you may even want to put them into a scrapbook or frame them.

You may also be hit with regret. It is possible to be relieved and sad at the same time. Perhaps you hoped that the abusers of your past had reformed and chosen better paths. You may have believed that, by now, they had turned their lives around and found a way to make positive contributions to society. Maybe, deep down inside, you had always hoped you would have the chance to make peace with them. Instead, you may find yourself having to deal with the opposite truth. You may not find the ending you were hoping for.

In your world, the bullying you experienced was all about you. You saw events through your own lens. It is possible you lacked the empathy to understand the other children's motivation for their behavior. Maybe the question of why people were tormenting you never crossed your mind, because you were so caught up in your own drama.

Those who hurt you when you were children might have done so in reaction to the pain they were experiencing. Perhaps they had a rough start in their lives. Maybe, in some cases, they were never able to heal.

If you come across unexpected news while you're searching for the bullies of your childhood, it's okay to feel mixed emotions. You don't have to apologize for feeling a sense of freedom and relief, if events have put their own period at the end of the sentence and permanently ended somebody's campaign of bullying against you. You're human, after all.

The People You Don't Choose to Find

You probably wouldn't be able to track down every class member in the time you want to devote to your search. Most likely, you will not want to find all of the people who hurt you in the past, anyway.

Some of them are not worth it. Former classmates may not merit your research time, because they were not among the leaders in the community of tormentors. They did not initiate the bullying but, instead, simply went along with the bad choices others made.

There might have been so many tormentors in your childhood that you didn't hold onto memories of them all. The most forgettable of them might have taken up so little space in your memories that you have only wispy recollections of them. That's probably about all of the energy they're worth.

There may have been others who caused you so much pain that you truly cannot look at them again, even with the screen of an electronic device to serve as a buffer. Some of them may awaken such torturous memories that you would not ever want to look at their online profiles.

People who hurt you physically or who pushed your emotional buttons with the most precision may well be people who you don't want to revisit under any circumstances. Don't chastise yourself up for it.

That does not make you a coward or someone who is leaving part of an important job undone. Rather, you are expending your energy on things that are most productive for you without forcing yourself to do anything that feels dangerous, threatening, or unhelpful. You don't have to retraumatize yourself in order to prove anything to yourself or anybody else.

CHAPTER ELEVEN

FACING YOUR FOES IN THE REAL WORLD

Telling your story; optimizing your online presence, and preparing yourself for the eventuality that the people from your past would contact you; and finding your foes online may go a long way toward bringing you healing. However, once you have accomplished those tasks, you may feel as if you still have unfinished business.

Viewing your childhood abusers online may have been difficult. But you knew, while you were researching your former tormentors, that you had privacy. No one had to know that you were looking for them. The bullies and their associates didn't receive any notification that you had found them.

Apart from the anguish of making contact with the monsters of your past, you were safe. There is a distinct line between the virtual world and the real world, and you stayed on one side of it. That may be the place where you should remain. If you have found relief from the past by facing it, then maybe you're done. You may have accomplished your goal and, if that is the case, then you don't need to proceed.

198 · STACEY J. MILLER

Perhaps, though, you aren't through yet. You may feel that you have unfinished business with your childhood adversaries.

Maybe you feel the need to face your foes in the real world in order to bring yourself lasting peace and closure. Facing the tormentors and others of your childhood will require courage, commitment, and the ability to deal with uncertainty.

Last time you encountered the abusers of your childhood, they were monsters who attacked you and did lasting damage to you. This time — if you open up the possibility of intersecting with the abusers of your past — it may not be a whole lot different. Some people don't mature significantly from childhood to adulthood.

The Case of Dr. Lance Hindt

An alleged case in point is Dr. Lance Hindt who was the Katy Independent School District (ISD) Superintendent. This is in the Houston, Texas area.

In March 2018, a man by the name of Greg Barrett attended a Katy ISD school board meeting. Barrett stepped up to the microphone and accused Hindt of bulling him when they attended junior high school together decades before. He claimed that the abuse he experienced was severe enough to make him contemplate suicide.

The confrontation at the school board meeting was captured on video and widely circulated on Reddit and beyond after the incident. The video shows Barrett emotionally recounting the abuse he claims to have suffered at the hands of Hindt. According to the ABC television affiliate in Houston,

Texas, the video also shows Hindt's apparent lack of response to Barrett's comments. Although some people viewing the video believe they hear laughter after Barrett speaks, there is no evidence that is what they were hearing. Someone else might have been laughing, or maybe that noise in the background isn't laughter at all.

At the same time, it seems clear that Hindt failed to apologize, show remorse, look embarrassed, or respond in any other way that Barrett might have been deemed appropriate. The video seems to show that Barrett walked away from the microphone without receiving any satisfaction from Hindt.

During the media coverage, Hindt denied Barrett's accusations about bullying. However, at least two other people — a man who claims to have witnessed the particular event that Barrett described at the meeting and another former high school classmate, Circuit Judge David Carpenter of Alabama's 10th district — came forward. They publicly recalled Hindt's bullying of children years before.

A very long time had passed between Hindt's childhood and his appointment as Katy ISD's Superintendent. Memories fade, and it's natural that individuals remember things differently. It may be that the only people who will ever know the whole truth about what happened then are Barrett and Hindt.

So we have no proof, other than Greg Barrett's word, that Dr. Lance Hindt harmed him. However, Barrett apparently attended the school board meeting to confront the person who he believes bullied him during their childhood.

His goal is a matter of conjecture. Maybe he wanted an apology from Hindt. It was possible that Barrett wanted to convey his opinion that the superintendent was unfit for the job. It also possible that Barrett wanted to humiliate Hindt in public to exact revenge.

Maybe Barrett simply wanted Hindt to acknowledge that hurting another child was wrong and that Barrett hadn't deserved to be tormented.

Possibly, Barrett felt the need to verbalize, for Hindt's benefit, what the consequences of his alleged bullying, decades before, had been. Maybe, since Hint was now in a position of authority with the Katy ISD, Barrett hoped to tug at his conscience and convince him to protect children in his jurisdiction from bullying. In any case, Barrett appeared to have achieved nothing in exchange for risking so much.

That story demonstrates the potential consequences you may encounter when you face your childhood tormentors in the real world. You may build up your courage and finally manage to articulate your darkest and most painful memories, the way that Barrett did ... and, like Barrett, you may be met with indifference, denial, or scorn. Instead of earning the reward you may deserve for your bravery, you stand to make things even worse for yourself.

If you decide to bring the past into the present, you are walking into uncharted territory. The consequences of your actions will be unknowable until they unfold. You may or may not achieve your goals. Perhaps you will gain only frustration and additional humiliation. That is the risk you take.

However, the story of Barrett and Hindt has a postscript.

In May 2018, two months after the confrontation with Greg Barrett, Hindt resigned from his position as Katy ISD's Superintendent.

His resignation was to take effect in January 2019. At the time of this writing, Hindt was still denying the charges that he was a bully during his childhood, and his school district supporters had filed a defamation lawsuit on his behalf.

Barrett may or may not have gotten any, or all, of what he wanted when he attended the school board meeting, and stepped up to the microphone, that day. But at least he raised his voice in protest of the abuse he claims he experienced. That, alone, might have been enough for him.

Additionally, though, he now has the satisfaction of knowing that the man he named as one of his tormentors will not have the last word. Hindt will not remain in the job where he probably did not belong, if Barrett's memory is reliable.

Weighing the Pros and Cons

You may want to do as Barrett did even though you can't know, ahead of time, how it will turn out. The potential benefits may outweigh the risks. That is something you will have to weigh for yourself.

History is immutable. What happened in your childhood cannot be changed. You can't rewrite the story of your past, but you may be able to shoot an alternate ending.

The pain you experienced at the hands of the bullies and their associates, and its effects on you, cannot be denied or eradicated. However, you may be able to add to the narrative and make it more palatable.

In other words, you could potentially justify putting yourself back in contact with the people who hurt you. Logistically, it would probably be relatively easy to do so.

You may welcome the opportunity to connect with the antagonists from your past. This would give you a chance to write a happier ending to the story. It may also provide you

202 · STACEY J. MILLER

with the closure you need to finally, and permanently, end the pain of your childhood bullying. And, for whatever it may be worth to you, your interaction may also benefit the perpetrators.

However, you are not obligated to find and face your abusers just because the internet has made it possible. It's no badge of honor to subject yourself to the potential for emotional, spiritual, or even physical re-injury. Only you can decide whether facing the abusers of your past is riskier than continually exerting the energy required to suppress, or replay, the terrible memories.

Taking the Next Steps

You have to determine for yourself which, if any, steps to take next. It may be helpful to seek the advice of a mental health counselor, family members, or friends before making your decision.

Facing the Bully in the Real World

You are not obligated to face your bully in the real world just because the internet may have made it possible. This is someone who once tormented you. Facing this individual again may be something you just don't want to do or feel you can't handle.

Subjecting yourself to the bully again may be the last thing you would find beneficial. If that's the case, don't do it. You have nothing to prove to anybody. Harming yourself will do nobody any good.

Only you know the intensity of your feelings and understand the range of your vulnerabilities. If your emotions are running high, and you feel as if a strong gust of wind could knock you over emotionally, then this is not the right time for you to approach your childhood abuser. Maybe the right time will never come. Don't push it and risk retraumatizing yourself.

It's possible the bully has not changed as much as you would hope, and that the two of you are in positions similar to the ones you occupied as children. You may still be hungering for the bully's approval, and your abuser may still crave power and control. Even now, the bully may be willing to get what he or she needs at your expense, if you provide him or her with the opportunity.

It will not help either of you to reenact an unhealthy relationship. It certainly would do you no good to expose yourself to further abuse. You know the old wisdom, which probably originated with Albert Einstein: the definition of insanity is doing the same thing but expecting different results.

There's a school of thought that says, while humans who suffered trauma are naturally predisposed to wanting to connect with their predators to try to rewrite history, it is always a bad idea to do so.

But we are talking about a former abuser who was a child at the time when your paths crossed. This is someone whose brain wasn't fully developed and who may not have had the capacity to understand the consequences of his or her bullying. It is possible the bully has matured into someone quite different from the person who once tormented you. Therefore, you may want to consider reaching out on the grounds that enough of the variables may have changed.

Also, leaving well enough alone may not be ideal if "well enough" is awful. You may not want to settle for the easiest solution, which is to maintain the status quo.

Instead, you may want to reach out to the bully. It may do you both some good to connect. While you can't change what happened in the past, you may be able to provide a different conclusion that would be easier to live with. The bully may want to atone for the mistakes he or she made. Perhaps you will want to open the door to allow that.

Creating an alternate ending won't erase the memory of the original. But it may give you a better narrative to lay alongside the old one. You may finally be able to let go of the pain, knowing that you have concluded your unfinished business and tied up loose ends.

Your life experience or studies in psychology may have taught you that you will keep reliving the same patterns until you resolve the issue. Until you face the bully of your childhood, you may be more susceptible to bullying in the workplace, in social relationships, and even when you're dealing with strangers in public.

Your religious convictions may tell you that extending an olive branch and offering forgiveness is simply the higher, and more honorable, road to take. Perhaps your spiritual beliefs hold that you will reincarnate endlessly until you successfully deal with the problem. If you adhere to either of those belief systems, then you may have an extra incentive to pursue facing your foes in the real world.

Dealing with the bully from the other side of your electronic device may allow you to shed that nagging feeling that you have left something undone or that you have unanswered questions. Maybe you just are tired of living in subtle, but real, fear that the bully is out there somewhere and could hurt you. You may crave the opportunity to release any power that the abuser may still have over you.

On a practical level, you probably can reach out online to the person who once bullied you without investing too much time, energy, or emotion in the process. You can make it relatively painless. The potential payoff — swapping out perpetual pain for peace — may outweigh the risks.

Your efforts may not deliver the results you want, though. It is impossible to predict what might happen.

Sometimes, little bullies grow up to become big bullies. On the other hand, sometimes childhood bullies grow into well-adjusted adults who wish they could change the past and undo the damage they caused.

The bully of your childhood may have grown into an unprincipled adult, or he or she may have acquired decency somewhere along the way. Maybe the truth lies somewhere in between. You can't know the type of person you will find in advance of reaching out.

You may have already found the bully online. Perhaps, according to what you have seen, this person seems capable of kindness. However, that does not necessarily mean that kindness is the individual's only —or even dominant — quality. The chemistry between the two of you may still be toxic. Or the bully might have manipulated his or her online profile to create someone who doesn't really exist or who only exists for some people. Maybe the online profile you've viewed suggests a far different person from the adult you would find if you reached out to him or her.

But if you let go of your expectations, and if you can be willing to accept that the bully's response to your overture would be a reflection of the bully rather than of you, then reaching out may be a reasonable action to take. It may offer you the best opportunity for lasting peace.

Connecting with your former bully is a choice with potentially serious pitfalls. If you are looking for an adventure, you may want to try white water rafting or mountain climbing instead. Don't do this for fun. It won't be.

However, if you have a specific goal in mind, then you may commit to getting in touch with your childhood tormentor. If so, proceed cautiously. Be respectful — toward yourself and toward the bully.

Just as you would not want the bully to jump out at you from behind some bushes and shout "surprise," you should not attempt to ambush the bully. Give the bully plenty of warning that you are there.

The kindest and most secure way to reach out to the bully is through a social network that he or she has joined. That makes getting in touch a two-step process (if you discount the third step, which you may already have taken, of finding the bully's social network profile).

To send in-network messages that have the best chance of getting through to the recipient, you usually must first receive the other person's tacit permission. That means there is a step you must take before you send a private email through social networks. You must first reach out to the other person, and that individual must accept your overture.

The logistics of taking that first step vary depending on the social network you choose, and that will probably be the one with which you feel the most comfortable. Only choose one social network through which to approach the bully. If the bully sees several invitations from you, from different social networks — however respectful those invitations might have been — that may strike him or her as creepy. You want the bully to see your gesture as inviting and positive rather than threatening, excessive, or odd.

All you are doing, at this point, is sending an invitation to connect on Facebook, LinkedIn, Twitter, or another social network. That social network will immediately relay the invitation to the recipient. Then it will notify you as soon as the bully accepts your invitation. Your job is to wait patiently.

You may receive a quick response. The bully may happen to see the notification soon after you've made an overture. Maybe the bully frequently checks, and responds to, social network notifications. When the bully sees an invitation from you, maybe the bully will drop everything to respond. On some level, maybe the bully has been waiting for you to get in touch for years.

If you do not receive an instant reply, don't jump to conclusions. A time lag in receiving a response could mean anything including: the bully checks that social network infrequently or never; your overture arrived when the bully was busy or on vacation; your name doesn't ring a bell; or you have surprised the bully, and he or she needs time to decide what to do.

Hearing nothing, after a reasonable interval has passed, probably means that the bully simply would prefer not to connect with you. If that's the case — if the bully can't, or won't, respond to your overture — then that is the bully's choice. Resist the temptation to push the issue. No means no, as the wisdom goes.

In that case, change your strategy. Contact another of your former antagonists instead, if you still feel the need to connect with one of the people who bullied you. Although the bully may not be willing to help you in your healing process, a close associate of the bully's may feel differently.

If the bully does accept your invitation, then you are now connected via that social network. Therefore, the bully can send you a message or post on your page (if your chosen privacy settings for that social network allow people to post on your page). And you can now send a message to the bully.

If the bully posts a message on your page, it may be best to bring the conversation out of the public realm and respond via a private message. It will be tough enough to connect in private with someone who abused you. The conversation that you may have as a result is probably not one that you want the public to see or hear. Protect your privacy, and the bully's, by taking your dialogue to a private virtual space.

It is more likely, now that you are connected via social media, that the bully will wait for you to toss the ball back over the wall. Do so by sending a private or direct message to the former antagonist.

It is also possible that the bully does not have a social network account. That will make things trickier. In that case, you can use a search engine to find the bully's email address.

That route is riskier, because sending an email is not a two-step process. You probably will have to send off the email without knowing how, or even by whom, it will be received. The bully will have no advance notice that you may be trying to get in touch.

For that reason, keep your initial (and, perhaps, your only) email as neutral as possible. Make it brief and simple. Explain who you are without interjecting any accusations or casting blame.

Your email may not go directly to the bully. The person who reads it first may be someone else entirely. Be respectful of that individual's feelings, and try not to cause harm to anyone.

Assure the person — whether it's the bully or not — who is reading the email that you have no wish to argue, create drama, or cause unpleasantness of any kind. Succinctly explain why you are reaching out. Perhaps there's something you want to ask, something you want to hear, or something you want to say.

Let the bully know how to reply. Perhaps you would prefer to receive an email, text message, or phone call.

To contact the bully initially, use only an email address that should go directly to the bully. Steer clear of any other accounts, such as a general business email address or one that is likely to be shared by several family members.

There is always doubt about the security of email addresses. Of course, there's the possibility of hacking, but that's outside of your control. More to the point, there's a good chance that family members, significant others, and coworkers have access to each other's email accounts. There's a risk that even an email account that looks as if it would only be read by the individual you're trying to reach may be available for others to see, too.

But if you come across an email address that is more dubious than usual — such as an "info at a domain name" type of address — then you should not use it. Emails with nameless and general addresses may be routed to multiple people.

You wouldn't want your email to embarrass the bully or raise questions. That would be as counterproductive as it would be unkind. Although you can't prevent your email from accidentally making its way to family members or coworkers, you don't want create an elevated risk by using an address unless you have a clear indication that only the bully uses the account.

The people who are currently part of the bully's life, including their family members, friends, and coworkers, were not part of your childhood. They did nothing wrong and don't deserve to be scripted into this part of the story, either. Keep your communication between the bully and you, to the extent that you can.

Explain your goal, and let the bully know your preference for achieving it. Do you want to exchange emails or text messages?

Perhaps you would prefer to arrange a phone call or a face-to-face meeting. That may strike you as more helpful, but don't try to force anything. Let this be a mutual decision.

Your purpose is to create an opportunity for a dialogue between two mature adults. Be as respectful and kind as you can to maximize your chances of success. Remember what you've heard about catching more flies with honey than with vinegar. It turns out to be true.

If you send an email, and you don't hear back — wait a couple of weeks, and then try once more. If you get no response, drop it.

The bully may be just as embarrassed about bullying you as you have been about being targeted. Give the bully time to think things through and space to act responsibly. Don't corner or rush the bully.

If the bully does respond, then listen carefully and deeply to what he or she has to say initially. You don't have to empathize with the bully, necessarily, but you should hear what this person has to say.

Try to find humanity in the response. You may be able to spot common ground. Maybe the bully has never talked about that part of his or her childhood, either. Perhaps the bully's behavior was a result of his or her own pain. You may be opening up old hurts for the bully, too.

The opportunity to have a dialogue can be positive for both of you. If the bully agrees, and you do arrange an encounter of some sort — via email, text, a phone call, or an in-person meeting — then here are some things to keep in mind during that conversation.

First, you have created an opportunity to heal. Be grateful that you were able to made it happen, regardless of the outcome.

You did a brave thing. Feel good about that, and most of all, be considerate toward yourself.

Your needs come first. Respect yourself, and accept nothing less than that from the bully. Secondarily, do your best to reciprocate. The bully may have done nothing, ever, to earn your respect. Provide it, anyway, because you're a big enough person to do so.

Be as sensitive as possible to the bully's feelings and needs without opening yourself up to developing Stockholm syndrome. This person is your former tormentor, not your former — or current — friend. His or her pain is not yours to bear. Don't let the bully turn the tables on you, intimidate you, or convince you that you did anything wrong.

If the bully says, or implies, that you should have been able to defend yourself, don't believe it. As an adult, you may be able to explain string theory, pilot an airplane, perform open heart surgery, or deal with some of the best emotional button pushers out there with absolute confidence and efficiency. But you couldn't do any of those things then. You were a child.

You don't have to accept the blame or the responsibility for what you did or what you didn't do back then. You have nothing to feel guilty about.

The bully should not have abused you. Whether or not he or she feels remorse for doing so is up to the bully. But accepting the blame for the bully's childhood choices is not your obligation. It never was, and it never will be.

Look for the bully's humanity as evidence that he or she is no longer a monster. The bully's personality defects or emotional problems are beyond your control. The bully may be damaged in ways that you can't repair.

Accept the bully's limitations, and respect the bully's boundaries. Don't let the bully's response to you determine how you feel about yourself.

You may already know what you want to convey when you meet with the bully, and you may have rehearsed saying (or keyboarding) it. But stay open to going off-script if it becomes necessary or desirable. Even though you may think you fully understand your reasons for getting in touch with the bully and the goals you want to achieve, you may surprise yourself by uncovering motives you didn't know were there.

Maybe you want to offer the bully forgiveness. Or maybe you want to find out why it happened, why the bully targeted you, how the individual feels about bullying now, what this person has told his or her own children about bullying, or whether the bully can assure you that he or she will never hurt you again.

Perhaps what you really need is to have the bully address one deep-seated fear you've struggled with, or say one key phrase. That may be all you need to understand that this is finally over so you can stop agonizing and move on.

If the bully has any questions for you, take all the time you need to hear, and process, them. Don't feel pressured to respond instantly. Think first.

Don't allow anger or the desire for revenge to derail the conversation. Hear your inner child, and be respectful of what that voice is telling you. But, more importantly, honor the guidance of your highest self.

Do the right thing, as you understand it. Don't let your heated passions overwhelm your good sense and lead the way. Instead, modulate the expression of your feelings. Behave responsibly, and make yourself proud.

Show the bully the compassion that he or she should have given you during your childhood. Focus on your desire to heal and find peace. Extend the opportunity for healing and finding peace to the bully, too. Create only positive energy and good karma, if you can.

Once you have faced the monster, you may feel as if you've just completed the Boston Marathon. You may feel more like collapsing than celebrating.

In the immediate aftermath, you may not even sense that a weight has lifted from you. Perhaps, instead, you will feel numb. You may need time to decompress and process your feelings. It may help if you talk to a friend, loved one, or mental health counselor.

Facing your bully in the real world may not be an instant fix. Instead, it may be like ripping an adhesive bandage off an open wound. It may hurt more before it feels better.

This may be one of the most difficult things you will ever do, but it also has the potential to be one of the most rewarding. Once you have met the bully in the real world and lived through the experience, you may finally be able to let the pain go. You may find the peace, and the closure, that you deserve.

Facing the Bully's Court in the Real World

If you've faced the bully already, then your job may be through. There may be no more monsters that you need to shrink down to their appropriate sizes.

However, the bully's closest childhood associates — members of the bully's court — also may loom as unfinished business for you.

Think of them as also-rans. They weren't the main bullies in your story, but they weren't far behind.

The pain they left in their wake, once you parted company with them, might have started out the size of a basketball. As time went on, it might have shrunk to the size of a tennis ball, then a ping pong ball, then a marble and, finally, a pea.

Perhaps, at this point, the pain that remains inside of you is no more than a minor nuisance. But maybe you find that no pain is acceptable.

That isn't unreasonable on your part. Why should you accept any hurt at all that the bully's court may still be causing you? You don't deserve to suffer, or to be inconvenienced, at all because of them.

You should be able to attend a class reunion, if you'd like, without worrying what will happen if you encounter the people at the top of your class' social hierarchy. You ought to be able to move through your life without fearing there may be landmines buried somewhere, with your name on them, just waiting to be detonated. You don't want anything lurking out there that may blow up and cause you harm.

Perhaps you have decided not to contact the bully. Maybe, in your estimation, the bully isn't worth the effort or the risk you would take by subjecting yourself to another encounter. It may be easier, and more reasonable, for you to reach out to the bully's court instead.

You may feel less emotional about them and better equipped to handle a potential encounter with the people who hung around with the bully and supported him or her, but who didn't initiate the campaign of bullying.

Perhaps you will be able to see the humanity in these former antagonists if you reach out to them. Maybe you can transform them from monsters into regular mortals and then disengage your emotions from them.

You don't have to like these people. In fact, once you make your peace with them, you never have to even give them another thought.

Maybe you can reach a place where you feel comfortable with the fact that they're sharing this planet with you. Even though you'll know they are out there still, perhaps that will no longer cause you any distress.

If you were not able to find the bully online, or else you couldn't find a secure email address to use, and you still want to try to contact the bully, the members of the bully's court may be able to help. One or more of the bully's former friends may still be in touch with him or her.

Once you've made contact with the court member, you may want to ask whether he or she would be willing to act as an intermediary for you. Maybe this individual would ask the bully to get in touch with you and vouch for the fact that you mean no harm.

You may feel that your request is reasonable and that helping you get in touch with the bully is the least a member of the bully's court owes you. Maybe you are correct.

Expect pushback, though. Members of that inner circle may retain a strong loyalty toward the bully. Despite the fact that he or she may acknowledge that the bullying was wrong, the court member may still prioritize protecting the bully over helping you.

That would not be the outcome you want, but it would be understandable. The bully was more than a bully during your childhood. He or she may also have served as a friend, leader, mentor, hero, ally, or teammate to others — particularly, to those who were part of the bully's inner circle. Those individuals may feel the bully earned their allegiance. You, on the other hand, were not their friend. Therefore, if you force the court members to decide between protecting their longtime friend and helping you, the outcome won't necessarily be the one you would want.

If you ask for the help of one of the court members in reaching out to the bully, and you receive a positive response, great. If not, your best bet would probably be to let it go. You had other classmates. Perhaps one of them would be willing to help.

Facing the Followers in the Real World

If you reach out to followers, keep your expectations in check. Time has elapsed since your childhood.

The followers probably didn't loom as large in your life during the difficult times as some of the children who were higher up in the pecking order of your classroom. You probably didn't matter all that much to them, either. Their memories of you may have faded.

They may have forgotten the fact that they hurt you. It may have been necessary for them to revise history and deemphasize the role they played. That may have enabled them to live with what they did.

Don't force your point of view on them if their perspective differs from yours. They are entitled to have their own version of reality. While truth is immutable, we can edit it to our advantage and tell ourselves what we must in order to get by.

The followers may have had to spin things a certain way to hold onto their self respect and move on with their lives. Allow them that.

You don't need to argue with the followers if they have forgotten what they did to you. Bringing that negativity into your life, or theirs, won't help anything.

But you may want to request an apology from the people who followed the lead of the bully in your class and caused you misery. You may find it helpful to ask why the followers made the choices that they did. Perhaps it would be helpful to hear what they were going through during their childhoods that led them to behave that way. Maybe, through listening, you will gain some insights that will help you process the past and make peace with it.

Facing the Silent Bystanders in the Real World

You may have no reason to contact those who saw that you were suffering and did nothing to help. However, if you are determined to cast your net far and wide, then getting in touch with some of those silent bystanders may be on your agenda.

Whether or not you decide to reach out to any of the silent bystanders, try not to judge them any more harshly than you must. Things were different when you were children. Bullying was ignored by nearly everyone then.

At that time, the silent bystanders probably didn't have access to a school resource officer or a school liaison. They didn't sit in on lectures about what to do if they saw someone being bullied. They read no pamphlets, and saw no videos, movies, or plays on the subject.

They were on their own.

Obviously, they weren't as alone as you were. But they lacked the educational and peer support for intervening in bullying that children may now receive. They may have wanted to do better, but maybe they didn't know the right thing to do or the right way to do it.

You don't have to forgive the silent bystanders. But it may be helpful to understand where they were coming from and to be grateful that, perhaps, there will be fewer silent bystanders to enable bullying in the future.

There are some things you may be able to learn from them by listening to what they have to say. Maybe they, too, will be grateful for the opportunity to connect.

Perhaps they will be pleased to hear that you are doing well. Maybe they will welcome the opportunity to make amends for their failure to help you or at least share how their choices may have affected them.

If one or more of the silent bystanders is generous enough to offer you some of their time, then you may benefit by accepting the opportunity to learn more ... and to further heal.

Facing the Converts in the Real World

There's no reason to sugarcoat it. Those who were once your friends and switched teams when it was more socially advantageous for them to do so made a huge mistake. Their abandonment of you amounted to nothing less than cowardice.

You may have little to say to the followers or silent bystanders, so you may choose to bypass them in the real world. However, you may feel differently about getting in touch with those with whom you once had a mutually caring relationship.

It comes down to making a choice. You can ignore the positive history that you shared with the converts and remember only the betrayal. Or you can focus on the good times you shared with the converts, and you can reach out to them in honor of that former friendship.

Either way, you don't have to overlook the harm that the converts did to you. You can remember everything — including the fact that, when you needed them, the converts deserted you. It's okay to recall that, when their support might have made all the difference, they withheld it.

You may believe that, if the converts ever really cared about you, they would have found a way to apologize at some point during the years. That may be a fair point.

On the other hand, perhaps the converts were so ashamed of their behavior that they just couldn't find a way. Maybe they wanted to and simply didn't know how.

You can't undo the harm they caused you, but you may be able to mitigate the damage they did by allowing yourself to remember the positive things about the people who once were your friends. The converts let you down. Still, they may hold

220 · STACEY J. MILLER

wonderful memories in their hearts that are worth unpacking and appreciating together.

It's possible that, before the abuse began, you were enjoying your school-related life, and the converts were a part of that world. You had friends, including them, and a sense of belonging. Things made sense. You may have suppressed even the best of your memories so that you wouldn't have to cope with the pain of the worst of them. Reaching out to the converts can help you reconnect with the parts of your childhood that weren't toxic. You may find that, together, you can rediscover some shared history that's worth rediscovering.

You're entitled to feel gratitude for the bright spots of your childhood and to remember all the reasons you once called the converts your friends. Don't expect to resume those friendships, because that may not be possible. You don't know what the converts were thinking then, and you can only guess what their feelings are now.

Regardless of how the converts react to your overture, though, you can still bathe emotionally in the positive nostalgia — even if it is one-sided. Remembering the friendship you once felt for each other, and embracing those memories, can be healing.

You can hope to bask in some of those memories together with the people you once called your friends. If that isn't possible, you can at least choose to cherish those memories alone. That privilege will be yours no matter what.

Facing the Other Targets in the Real World

While you were suffering abuse, you might have picked on other people who were the bully's targets. Or you might have failed to provide them with the support they could have used when you had a chance.

Maybe, now, you want to reach out to the other targets and express your regret for the mistakes that you made. You can't know how they will react.

It is your right to hope that your words will have some therapeutic value for the other targets. But offering you forgiveness is not their moral imperative.

The other people who suffered bullying that you might have been able to mitigate are under no obligation to even give you the time of day. Some things are beyond forgiving. The fact that you, too, were bullied was not an excuse to behave horribly or to stand by while other children did.

However, you have the right to reach out to the other former targets to make amends. You may find it helpful to say you are sorry.

It may terrify you to reach out to someone you mistreated or did not support. But try to work through that, because the other targets deserve the effort.

Doing the right thing isn't always easy. You may feel that apologizing to the other former targets will lift a burden of guilt from your shoulders, regardless of how your overture is received.

The other former targets have the option of receiving your apology without forgiving you, if that's what is best for them. They can appreciate your gesture and your courage. Perhaps they will want to accept your apology.

Be aware, though, that you may have waited too long. However sincere you are in your remorse, it may have come too late. The children you hurt may be long gone, and the adults those children grew into may not be in a position to

222 · STACEY J. MILLER

accept your apology. Even if forgiveness falls beyond the
scope of what they can offer you, they may still benefit from
your gesture.

The other former targets may also appreciate the opportunity to share their feelings about watching the bullying you
endured. Perhaps they, too, have always regretted their inability to do anything to help you. Maybe, together, you can
process the pain of what you experienced.

If you have found productive ways to address the past, you
may want to share them with the other former targets. Helping
others provides some of the greatest opportunities of all to
heal.

Facing the Teachers and Coaches in the Real World

The teachers and coaches, theoretically, should have been
in charge of your everyday school life. At some point, though,
they surrendered their authority to your abusers. While you
suffered, they looked the other way. They saw nothing. They
heard nothing. They did nothing.

Or worse, they participated in the bullying. They egged on
your tormentors. In either case, they abdicated their responsibility to care for you and to protect you. They let you down. If
they served as models at all, they were examples of what
teachers and coaches should not be.

Perhaps, by now, your former teachers and coaches have
built thriving careers in fields outside of education, or they
may have retired. If so, great. You may have no reason to contact them.

However, they may still be teaching or coaching. They
may even have moved up the career ladder in the same, or
another, school system. In that case, you may have something

to say to them. It may be a good idea to ask them to treat any students who are currently in their care better than they did you.

You may want to remind them about what they failed to do. It's fair enough for you to tell them about the pain they caused you and convey the long-term effects it has had on your life.

Also, review their school's anti-bullying and anti-cyber bullying policies, as well as state laws and regulations that may apply. You can find them online by beginning at the government anti-bullying site, StopBullying.gov. Familiarize yourself thoroughly with what teachers and coaches are now legally obligated to do to prevent, and address, bullying and cyber bullying inside, and beyond, the classroom.

Then feel free to offer the teachers and coaches your perspective about where they went wrong, and what you expect them to do differently now. The challenge will be to express your wisdom respectfully so that they won't dismiss it out of hand. The better informed you are, and the more confident and authoritative you appear, the greater the chance that the teachers and coaches will see the value of what you have to offer.

Your feedback may help the next generation of children in their care. Knowing that you hold them accountable for their past mistakes may induce them to try harder now.

Facing the Administrators in the Real World

If the school administrators are still employed in the world of education, and if their current positions are similar to the ones they held when you were a student, then it may be difficult for you to rest easy.

224 · STACEY J. MILLER

Anti-bullying and anti-cyber bullying policies, laws, and regulations are now in place. Administrators supposedly are better trained, and better equipped, to protect students than they were before. There are programs designed to prevent bullying and cyber bullying, and to enable those who work at schools to appropriately respond to it. The plan probably includes getting children involved in changing the school's culture so that bullying and cyber bullying are no longer acceptable, laudable, or cool.

The school now may have cameras and security officials in place. If there is an incipient problem, administrators will probably be able to handle it quickly and effectively.

They almost certainly have implemented zero tolerance policies. Absent evidence to the contrary, you can expect that the administrators are enforcing them.

Try not to lose sleep over the fact that the people who let you down the most during your childhood are still in positions of authority. They may not have grown more compassionate or competent with time, but — in the context of bullying — their personal qualities may matter less than they did.

School administrators are no longer solely in charge of addressing the problem of bullying. Now they have help from law enforcement.

They also have an accountability that they formerly lacked. Since bullying is no longer a dirty secret, school administrators know that they may potentially face lawsuits if they fail to protect the children in their care.

This is all to the good.

The school administrators who were willing to let you suffer probably have not undergone massive character transformations. They probably will still opt to take the path of least resistance, to the extent that is possible. It is likely they don't care a whole lot more about the children who are now in their care than they did about you.

However, society has changed. You now can expect administrators to protect their students from bullying. If they fail to do so, then students or parents can escalate the matter by bringing it to the local police department.

Once that happens, bullying is in the hands of the police officers and out of the hands of school administrators. You may find that to be a comforting development.

If you have any questions about how the school handles bullying and cyber bullying, then face the school administrators in the real world. Email them, and share your concerns. If they are wise and politically savvy, they will come up with answers that will help you find peace.

Facing Your Family in the Real World

It may be that your nuclear family lives in, or near, the neighborhood where you went to school even though you moved away. If that's the case, you may resist the idea of going home because of the possibility you will run into former bullies there.

As you heal, the fear of running into the abusers of your past may diminish. That can make it easier to get together with your family members on their turf.

Parents, siblings, grandparents, aunts, uncles, cousins, and extended members of your family should have been the people closest to you during your childhood. The bullying you experienced then might have driven a wedge between you, though, and that separation may have increased with time.

226 · STACEY J. MILLER

If you still have any of those individuals in your life, consider yourself lucky. Embrace the fact that you no longer have to keep the secret of your bullying from your family members. Tell them your story, if you think it can bring you closer. Let them into that part of your life. Allow them to grieve with you. Accept their willingness to help you recover, if they extend that to you.

Families are seldom perfect. You may have family members whose relationship with you is too toxic to embrace. If that's the case, then don't. There's no need. "Family" doesn't mean "obligated, no matter what."

Celebrate your relationship with the others, and focus on all the positive things that you can bring to one another.

Facing Your Salvation in the Real World

The saviors of your childhood might once have been regular mortals. They might have been children who instinctively knew the right thing to do and couldn't, under any circumstances, be persuaded to do otherwise. Or they might have been teachers, coaches, librarians, nurses, or counselors who acknowledged your humanity and offered you a reprieve from the suffering you experienced.

They might not have been able to spare you from the full effects of the bullying. The scope of what they could do to help you might have been limited.

Maybe all they could do was smile at you when you passed them in the hall, exchange a few words with you before classes began, or offer you a seat next to them on the school bus. Those gestures, which might have come naturally to them, were apparently not possible for so many of their peers. The fact that they could treat you with kindness and *compassion* means that they were your saviors, and the contributions they made to your childhood are worth honoring.

There is no greater joy than reaching out to the heroes of your childhood to express your gratitude. Acknowledging the people who supported you is a privilege.

There is no higher honor than to let the heroes in your life know what they meant to you in your childhood and to tell them that you will never forget them. There is no better feeling than to allow yourself to say thank you.

Reconnecting with those who saved you can be a wonderful experience. On the other hand, it can also have surprising results.

It is possible that the people who were your salvation don't remember what they did for you. In fact, they may not remember anything about that time in their lives. The school you attended was an unsafe place for you, and that might have been true for them, too. Your salvation might have experienced their own difficulties, and they might have needed to block out their memories.

Their actions, which seem so monumental to you, may not have been memorable at all to them. In their eyes, perhaps they were simply doing the right thing.

Of course, it is possible they remember you and have hoped that you would someday overcome the bullying of your childhood. They may have been sending you their good wishes, silently, through the years.

In either case, do get in touch with them, if you can. If they are no longer on this planet, honor them in your heart. Do something good in their name. Let the world continue to be a better place because they were in it.

AFTERWORD

This is not how I planned to close this book, nor is it how I wanted it to end. But fate took an unexpected turn.

While this book was in the editing stage, I saw a Facebook post from an old acquaintance announcing that a former classmate, Florence [which is a pseudonym], had passed away. Several other Facebook friends confirmed it.

The news stunned me. As I tried to process it, two Florences rushed into my head simultaneously.

Florence number one was an 11-year-old whom I'd met at the junior high school I had attended in Simmet. She was in my division in both seventh and eighth grades.

That Florence was the leader of the trio of pre-teen girls who launched the campaign of bullying against me.

When I had started junior high school, eager to explore my new surroundings and yet clueless about the culture around me, she had pounced on me. Florence, with her two cohorts, mercilessly tormented me.

As the school year wore on, she had recruited everyone within her sphere of influence to join in. The bullying was constant, and it was relentless. Florence called all of the shots, and she seemed determined to destroy me.

In many ways, she succeeded. Florence's actions, and my response to her behaviors, rerouted my life.

Florence's name was one of the first I searched for when social networking came to be. While I didn't want to face Florence online, or anywhere else, it was bound to happen sooner or later ... so I took the proactive approach of looking for her.

Despite my profoundly deficient facial recognition skills, I was able to identify Florence's photo quickly. That face had haunted me for decades. Ironically, the picture she had posted on Facebook was nearly identical to the one I'd carried in my mind all those years.

Looking at the photo hurt so much, at the time. I saw the face, and I remembered nearly all of the abuse she set in motion. As a matter of fact, I still do. I probably will never forget.

However, I no longer feel the need to bury those memories. I've worked through them. Florence and I dealt with them together.

As the memory of the first Florence filled my head, thoughts of a second Florence emerged, too.

The second Florence sent me a private message via Facebook nearly seven years ago. I didn't know what to expect when I saw the name with the familiar photo attached to it, and I felt terribly threatened by the possibilities.

No one from that part of my life had been in touch with me for about 33 years. Yet I had known the day would come when one of the bullies from my past would contact me, and I had prepared myself. I'd even maximized the chances that it could happen so that I would be the one in the driver's seat.

My online footprint was as large as I could make it. I had taken control of my online presence as well as anyone could. What people would find when they searched for my name was what I wanted them to see. Also, I had rehearsed that moment when someone from that part of my past inevitably found me on the internet and reached out to me.

Still, when it actually happened, it took all the courage I had to read what Florence had written. Her terse initial message asked if I were the Stacey Miller who had gone to such-and-such a junior high school in Simmet between 1975 and 1977. It seemed clear that the person who had sent me that message either was scared spitless, or she was coiled tightly and ready to spring at me.

I had no way of knowing which it was. After weighing my options — to respond or ignore her — I calculated that my failure to get back to Florence wouldn't make her go away. It might only encourage her to seek another, perhaps more intrusive, avenue of reaching me.

The pre-teenager inside of me pleaded for my protection. I felt her pain, but the adult in me needed to confront the monster so that I could move on.

It took me a full 24 hours, and countless rewrites of my original draft, to send Florence this reply: "Yes. Why do you ask?" Clicking on the "Send" button felt like a major accomplishment.

Florence responded within a few hours to say that she wasn't sure I would remember her and very much hoped that I did not. But, in the event that I did, she wanted me to know that she remembered me, too. Throughout the years, she had thought of me hundreds of times. Immediately after junior high school had ended, she'd realized what she had done. She had always wanted to get in touch with me to let me know how much she regretted everything.

She was not presuming to ask me for forgiveness, Florence continued, because she understood she didn't deserve that. But she had felt regret for so many years, and she didn't want to suffer in silence anymore. She asked me to acknowledge receipt of her message, because she thought it might provide her with some comfort to know that I had at least heard her remorse.

The intensity of Florence's feelings were evident in that second message, so I responded within a few hours via an email that I carefully crafted.

I told Florence that I well remembered the interlude we had experienced together; therefore, I fully appreciated the courage it had taken for her to reach out to me. I suggested that she work on forgiving herself.

We had attended a troubled junior high school at a terrible time, I reminded her. The teachers and administrators who were supposed to protect us then had let us down. In the absence of adult supervision and boundaries, we had both made mistakes.

I added that we were relatively lucky. We had survived those times and were able to trade messages. Phoebe Prince and her classmates would never have that privilege.

That seemed to resonate with Florence. She sent a message back to me quickly, and I replied. Within half a dozen messages or so, we switched to chatting online in real time.

A day or two after she first reached out to me, we friended each other on Facebook. Mostly through that venue, we kept up with what was going on in each other's lives.

We traded memories in spurts and sorted them out together. Via Facebook's Messenger program and, later, via telephone, we shared our mutual regrets, terrors, and hopes.

That second Florence was a warm, thoughtful woman with whom I found many points of connectivity. More than once, I asked for her thoughts about some problem that was perplexing me, and she generously provided it. I genuinely valued her advice, because her perspective was so very different from mine.

We kept saying we would get together in person, one of these days. I believe we meant it.

Mostly, we kept in touch online. Phone calls were infrequent, but our bond was undeniable.

It had been a month since I had heard from Florence online. I had planned, when my book was completed and edited, to send her a copy. I wanted her feedback, of course. Also, I hoped that she would agree to write a postscript to the book since she was such an integral part of my story.

Mostly, it seemed important to give her an opportunity to tell her side of the story, since I had told mine. She would have wanted to have that chance, I believe.

Florence wasn't a monster; she'd only played one in junior high school. She'd had her reasons. They didn't justify her actions. Nothing could. But the circumstances of her childhood went a long way toward explaining why she had worked so hard to wreck my world.

Most importantly, for her and for me, those reasons were in the distant past. We had both moved on.

Because I had been writing about her, Florence had been on my mind frequently. As I had nearly concluded the editing of this book, I thought about her even more. The time was rapidly approaching when I would get in touch with her. Unfortunately, that time never arrived. Her death intervened. So it's up to me to conclude this book by myself. This feels terribly wrong to me. But this is the way it has to be, so I will do what needs to be done and finish now.

Florence — both of the Florences I knew — changed my life. The first Florence engineered the brutal ending of my childhood. The second Florence took responsibility for her part in the tragedy and helped me to heal.

Our communication, as adults, enabled me to reframe what had happened during our childhoods. Florence had wanted to accept one hundred percent of the blame for what went wrong, but I wouldn't allow that then. I will not hear of it now, either.

Bullying wasn't the fault of the children who participated in it. It was the responsibility of the adults who failed to safeguard those children — all of them, including the bullies and their targets.

Now, as I struggle to process the loss of someone I considered a friend (ours was a *belated* friendship, I once told Florence), I see both Florences so clearly. I will forever grieve over the way in which I ran into the first Florence, and I will always be grateful for the grace that brought the second Florence into my world and gave us another chance.

Florence, if these words make their way to you somehow, please know this. There was never any way I could have forgiven you, even if you had asked that of me. There never was anything to forgive.

We were simply two people who were in a horrible situation, in an awful place, at a terrible time. Our collision was as inevitable as it was traumatic — not just for me, but for both of us.

You once told me that, if you could climb into a time machine and change the past, you would. I didn't respond then — I couldn't, because I was crying, and I didn't want you to know — but I want to do so now. Florence, I would gladly have held your hand and gotten into that time machine with you.

You and I both made mistakes when we were children, and that caused both of us so much suffering. The hurting child you were shouldn't have tormented me, and the child I was should have thought to ask you the magic question — why? Your answer might have changed everything.

We chose to do what we did, and we took responsibility for our actions long ago. We both worked hard to learn from them and move past them, and we succeeded in many ways.

Thank you, Florence, for giving us both the opportunity to write an alternate ending to our story. The second Florence — like the first Florence, so many years ago — initiated it all. This book wouldn't have been possible without you.

ACKNOWLEDGEMENTS

Paul Amirault, thank you for being my mentor, spiritual guide, muse, and wonderful friend. I couldn't have done this without you, and I wouldn't have wanted to.

Robert Carolan and John Publicover, you have been there since the beginning of my life and have always been part of it. Thank you for keeping the best of my childhood memories safe for all those years. I treasure you both.

Claire Davon, you've been a friend nearly forever as well as the sounding board that helped to make this book possible. Thank you.

Steve Bennett, for letting me share everything with you: my love and thanks.

Dr. Lynn R. Webster, thank you for pointing me to the research on the consequences of childhood trauma and for demonstrating the finer points of empathy, patience, and compassion that made this journey possible.

Ellen Walser deLara, PhD, MSW, author of *Bullying Scars*, you helped so much by writing a book about the aftermath of childhood bullying. Thank you for treating the subject with the gravitas it deserves.

My deep gratitude goes out to Doreen Weaton for her kindness, caring, and proofreading skills. Thank you, also, to Kristine Hanson and Steve Bennett for co-creating a cover that makes me smile.

To Rose Pavone, who showed fearlessness and leadership when I most needed to see that in a teacher, thank you. My high school community was more wonderful to me than I can begin to articulate. My thanks go out to all of its members, and especially to Bill Gregory, Father Michael Regan, and Bill Kemeza.

Barry Kipnes, thank you for helping with my research and, generally, being one of my favorite people on the planet. Thank you, too, for bringing your wonderful wife, Ferma, into my life. Howie and Betty Kipnes, I love you, too.

To the members of the Facebook group, Survivors of Bullying at School, you informed every one of this book's pages. Thank you for your trust, and sharing your experiences and insights.

To Mark Zuckerberg, you made healing and finding closure possible for so many of us. Thank you.

ABOUT THE AUTHOR

Photo by Steve Bennett

Stacey J. Miller is an independent book publicist, writer, editor, and social media strategist. Founder of S. J. Miller Communications, she is based in a suburb of Boston, Massachusetts.
Visit her online at www.bookpr.com.

Printed in Great Britain
by Amazon